UNSUSTAINABLE INEQUALITIES

UNSUSTAINABLE INEQUALITIES

Social Justice and the Environment

LUCAS CHANCEL

Translated by Malcolm DeBevoise

The Belknap Press of Harvard University Press

CAMBRIDGE, MASSACHUSETTS   LONDON, ENGLAND   2020

First printing

Library of Congress Cataloging-in-Publication Data

Names: Chancel, Lucas, author. | DeBevoise, M. B., translator.
Title: Unsustainable inequalities : social justice and the environment /
Lucas Chancel; translated by Malcolm DeBevoise.
Other titles: Insoutenables inégalités. English
Description: Cambridge, Massachusetts : The Belknap Press of
Harvard University Press, 2020. | First edition published in
French as Insoutenables inégalités: Pour une justice sociale et
environnementale. Paris : Les Petits Matins, Institut Veblen, 2017. |
Includes bibliographical references and index. |
Identifiers: LCCN 2020011098 | ISBN 9780674984653 (cloth)
Subjects: LCSH: Social justice. | Environmental justice. |
Equality—Economic aspects. | Economics—Sociological aspects.
Classification: LCC HM671 .C47413 2020 | DDC 303.3 / 72—dc23
LC record available at https://lccn.loc.gov/2020011098

CONTENTS

UNSUSTAINABLE INEQUALITIES

Introduction

THERE IS A CERTAIN tension between reducing socioeconomic inequalities and protecting the environment. For the most part these two objectives are compatible and often mutually reinforcing; but they may also be at odds with each other, as our political leaders do not tire of reminding us. Donald Trump, after all, justified his decision to leave the Paris Agreement on climate change on the ground that the jobs of American miners should be protected. Whatever his real motivation may have been (and one may reasonably suspect that it was neither the protection of American workers nor the health of Americans), the argument that environmental policy can improve the lot of a nation's poorest people deserves to be given a fair hearing.

If we are to avoid having to sacrifice one of these objectives in order to achieve the other, we must understand exactly why reducing inequalities is inseparable from the attempt to fundamentally alter our relationship to the environment. Otherwise it will be impossible to work out what must be done to reform current social and environmental policies and to implement a Green New Deal, as progressive political leaders are advocating around the world.

Recent studies in economics, political science, and epidemiology have shown that unless economic inequality is reduced, it will be extremely difficult to attain the other goals of sustainable development: democratic vitality, social well-being, economic efficiency, and ecological stability. The increasing levels of economic inequality observed in most Western countries today are therefore troubling not only in themselves, but also in view of the difficulties they create in realizing the aims of sustainable development in its most general sense.

The destruction of the environment, generally thought of as a harm handed down by one generation to the next, also exacerbates social inequalities within generations. It therefore has the effect of strengthening preexisting imbalances, which vary from country to country. The whole world is exposed to the risks associated with chemical pollution in the United States or in India, for example, but not every country is affected in the same way. In all countries, however, the relationship between environmental inequalities and economic inequalities resembles a vicious circle.

In the North and South alike, the rich are generally less exposed to environmental risks (pollution, climate-related misfortunes, fluctuations in the cost of natural resources, and so on) than the poor, who do not have the means either to protect themselves against them or to recover when disaster strikes. The catastrophe visited upon New Orleans by Hurricane Katrina in 2005 furnished a tragic example of what happens when rich and poor do not have the same degree of resilience in the face of calamity. The injustice of environmental inequalities mechanically reinforces the injustice of socioeconomic inequalities: deteriorating health due to pollution, or, in the case of natural disaster, to the destruction of places where people live and work, makes the situation of the most impoverished still more precarious and, as a consequence, worsens their position in relation to the rest of society. The dynamic at work here has aptly been called a poverty-environment trap.

To this vicious circle must be added another, arising from the unjust allocation of responsibility for environmental damages. Contrary to what certain authors maintain, it is not true that, beyond a certain level of income, people seek to reduce their level of pollution because they can afford to do so. With only rare exceptions, it is the wealthiest whose ecological imprint is the greatest. To use the technical term, there is no environmental Kuznets curve—no rise in the level of pollution up to a certain level of income, followed by a decline once this threshold is reached, at which point the environment begins magically to be protected. Socioenvironmental injustice is therefore twofold and symmetric: the biggest polluters are typically the ones who are least affected by the damages they cause.

It must also be kept in mind that those who suffer most from environmental degradation are often those whose voices are least heard when it comes to deciding the fate of the environment; they are also the ones who are most affected by environmental protection measures that do not take their interests directly into account. Critics of policies that are sometimes objected to, legitimately or not, as instruments of bohemian bourgeois ("bobo") environmentalism are right in any case to call attention to these basic facts.

But isn't all this well known and documented? Well, no—or at least not yet known and documented well enough! We are now beginning to have some insight into the underlying problems. But citizens, activists, and elected officials still have much more to learn about the connections between environmental inequalities and socioeconomic inequalities. Too often public debate ends once the potentially inegalitarian effects of enacting a tax on the carbon content of fossil fuels (a "carbon tax") or other climate measures have been more or less summarily discussed. To be sure, these proposals raise questions of income and wealth redistribution that must be carefully considered. But there are other crucial issues that need to be examined as well. How much do we really know about the disparate effects on individuals and populations of climate change, water pollution, or soil contamination? How much do we really know about the level of investment in infrastructure for public transportation and energy production that will be required if we are to protect the environment while at the same time reducing socioeconomic inequalities? We still sorely lack the empirical data and analytical tools—and sometimes the will and financial resources as well—that will be needed in order to fully understand the complex interactions between environmental and socioeconomic inequalities. But knowing and understanding are not enough. We must also be able to remedy these injustices. In this respect, and especially with regard to political implementation, we are still a long way from being able to do what needs to be done.

Putting social justice at the heart of the campaign for sustainable development means that the social and environmental policies presently in place in both industrialized and developing countries will have to be overhauled. It may seem odd, at first glance, that proposals for protecting the environment should often be criticized for not sufficiently taking into account the situation of the world's poorest people. Over the long term, disadvantaged populations stand to benefit the most from environmental protection. In the short term, however, measures that are conceived independently of policies aimed at improving social justice are liable to exacerbate certain inequalities and, indeed, to create new ones. Industrial polluters routinely threaten to eliminate jobs if stricter environmental regulations are enforced, for example, just as elected officials from rural constituencies protest the adoption of carbon taxes favoring city dwellers. Such arguments have been heard in the context of Green New Deal proposals in the United States and elsewhere. While they are often used cynically, they deserve attention. Is there a way to resolve the apparent contradiction between social justice and environmental protection?

I believe there is. But reconciling the two objectives will require a new approach to managing the social state that depends on the collective acceptance of responsibility for socioeconomic risks such as unemployment, sickness, and poverty. In order to integrate responsibility for major environmental risks (exposure to pollution and increases in the cost of natural resources, especially energy) with traditional mechanisms of social protection, it will be both desirable and feasible to move forward on three fronts.

To begin with, we must develop new tools for measuring and mapping environmental inequalities. The first step in solving a problem is having a clear view of it and being able to reliably monitor further developments. The key indicator of progress still today, in spite of many attempts to substitute a more informative measure for it, remains gross domestic product (GDP)—and this at a moment when researchers are capable of studying a far broader range of interacting factors. With regard to the production, dissemination, and sharing of data concerning environmental inequalities, for example, the United States was until quite recently ahead of many European countries. Even so, the executive branch often found it difficult to translate policy into effective action, and now it has openly abandoned its longstanding commitment to cooperating with other nations in addressing the problem of climate change.

Sophisticated methods for measuring inequalities are not enough. Political practices and bureaucratic organization will have to be transformed as well. It will be necessary in particular to decompartmentalize public policy, which historically has been constructed on a principle of strict separation between, on the one hand, government departments having specific responsibility for the environment and, on the other, departments dealing with the economy and financial affairs. A few countries have shown the way forward. In Sweden, for example, social assistance to poor households takes into consideration the constraints imposed by spending on energy (expenses associated with replacing obsolete and inefficient heating equipment and insulation, or costs of commuting for some individuals who live far from where they work).

Second, the traditional objectives of social policy need to be aligned with new measures for protecting the environment. Social inequality can be reduced in many ways, but governments must be mindful that the policies they choose between will have more or less desirable environmental consequences. Here again promising examples may be found in different parts of the world, even if their lasting effects are not always guaranteed. In the Canadian province of British Columbia, a carbon tax was introduced along with cash transfers to individuals based on their income level. In this way it became possible to protect the environment while ensuring that low-income individuals do not pay a disproportionate price. In Indonesia, until recently, about a quarter of the national budget was dedicated to subventions for environmentally harmful fossil fuels that chiefly benefited the car-owning urban middle and upper classes. The government abolished these subventions and used the savings to create a vast program of social protection aimed at reducing inequalities. In each of these jurisdictions we are witnessing the birth of a social and ecological state.[1]

Third, and finally, it will be necessary to devise new methods of collaboration between the social state and local governments in addressing the problems created by socioenvironmental inequality. Some activists call for a sense of joint responsibility to be promoted at the local level, in "transitional" towns and villages (to use the term favored by one of the most influential present-day movements in Europe). This view is partly correct. Environmental problems are often specific to particular places: soil contamination in certain rural districts, inadequate thermal insulation in the buildings of certain urban neighborhoods, the absence of public transportation in certain small towns, and so on. In order to correct these deficiencies while acting in close cooperation with the people who are most immediately affected by them, the best solution will be to mobilize the energies of individuals and private associations as well as the powers of municipal and regional councils. Nevertheless, it would be extremely unwise to count on local communities being able to do everything, for they themselves are apt to reproduce national forms of inequality on a smaller scale and in many cases are ill-equipped to meet the most pressing challenges of the coming decades. Local resources will therefore need to be supplemented by the authority of the social state. Here again, examples of successful cooperation among people and institutions at different levels of society can be found in many places—by no means all of them in Europe and North America.

Taken together, these new directions in social and environmental policy have the power to completely transform the welfare function of the state as it has traditionally been conceived. Other developments of immense significance must also be taken into account—globalization, the digital revolution, new threats to democratic stability—which complicate the task enormously. The good news, however, is that the ecological transition is already underway to one degree or another in many parts of the world. As we will see in the pages that follow, both industrialized and emerging countries have to learn not only from past mistakes but also from current successes, in the South no less than in the North. It goes without saying that transforming public policy on a global scale will require a massive and concerted effort on the part of people everywhere. Nevertheless, there is every reason to suppose that it is in fact possible—for it is actually taking place now.

PART ONE

The Sources of Unsustainable Development

1

Economic Inequality as a Component of Unsustainability

THE RESOUNDING success of French economist Thomas Piketty's *Capital in the Twenty-First Century*, a massive work on the dynamics of inequality, marked a turning point in contemporary economic debate.[1] The increase in inequalities of various kinds is now at the center of political debate as well. In 2013, Barack Obama called the rise in income inequality the "defining challenge of our time."[2] Institutions that had not previously been known for their egalitarian sympathies began to warn against the levels of inequality reached in both developed and developing countries. The International Monetary Fund, the World Bank, the Organisation for Economic Co-operation and Development (OECD), and even the World Economic Forum, an assembly of powerful interests convening every year in Davos, Switzerland, have frankly recognized that these inequalities constitute one of the gravest challenges to capitalism today.[3]

We will see in what follows that there is no consensus about the causes of this phenomenon and, as a consequence, no agreement about appropriate remedies. Nevertheless, the necessity of reducing inequalities is today unanimously admitted, something that was not the case only a few years ago. Translating this opinion into a program of concerted action, or at least the beginnings of one, took the form of setting target levels for the reduction of inequalities as part of the sustainable development goals (SDGs) laid out by the United Nations in its 2030 Agenda for Sustainable Development, adopted by all UN member states in fall 2015. The aim of this initiative is to make it possible for humanity to enjoy economic prosperity while at the same time protecting the environment against catastrophic degradation—and this in fewer than twenty years.

The Surprise of Rio

Three years earlier, in 2012, a conference called "Rio + 20" had been held in Rio de Janeiro. The name recalled the international summit meeting on sustainable development held in the Brazilian city in 1992, which inaugurated, among other things, a cycle of global conferences on the climate. By 2012, the time had come to assess the results of twenty years of economic development and environmental policies on a worldwide scale. It was in this context that the SDGs came into being. They were meant to supersede two political processes that until then had been distinct, by integrating them: implementation of the millennial development goals (MDGs), dedicated to combatting extreme poverty in developing countries, and successive rounds of international environmental negotiation now constituted a single plan for action.

The SDGs were novel for at least two reasons. First, they brought together the environment, the economy, and social policy, domains that had become largely disconnected over the past twenty years. The international community, either from an overriding concern for efficiency or an inability to deal with problems in a coordinated fashion, was used to treating trade issues (through the annual arbitration conferences of the World Trade Organization) separately from climate negotiation (through the cycle of international conferences on climate change) and the issue of poverty (isolated as an MDG). The SDGs, by contrast, are not limited to protecting the environment or to reducing extreme poverty: their declared aim is to achieve a high level of health and prosperity in every domain. These goals, seventeen in number, include some ten ancillary objectives (subgoals) ranging from eco-system restoration and an end to violence against women to a reduc-tion in infant mortality, universal access to the internet, and improving the quality of life in densely populated cities. The scope of this agenda is both a strength and a weakness.

The other innovation of the SDGs is that they are universal. Whereas the MDGs involved only developing countries, these goals apply to all countries, small or large, industrialized, emerging, or developing. This is quite remarkable and deserves to be emphasized: rich nations have swallowed at least some of their pride and accepted, or pretended to accept—I shall return to this point in due course—that the interna-tional community as a whole should have a say in determining the course of their own development. The "end of history"—the ultimate stage of liberal democracy theorized by the political scientist Francis Fukuyama—has therefore not yet arrived: all countries, including Western democracies meeting in Rio in 2012, realized that they still had a ways to go before reaching true prosperity.[4]

The American social scientist David Le Blanc has carefully studied the official resolutions establishing the SDGs in the hope of discovering the central aim that this sprawling agenda seeks to achieve.[5] From his analysis it becomes apparent that the goal of reducing inequalities of wealth, gender, power, and access to resources stands out among a net-work of more or less closely interrelated targets. It is intended as a catalyst, so to speak, for achieving the other objectives.

The first subgoal, under the head of "Inequalities," is to narrow in-come gaps within individual countries by 2020. The reduction of eco-nomic inequality is therefore seen to be central to the project of sus-tainable development—at least in the official version endorsed by the international community a few years ago. More precisely, the aim is to assure that the poorest 40 percent of the world's population will see their income increase more rapidly than the average. It is not a per-fect measure: some will object that it is an indicator of poverty (since it is limited to the poorest 40 percent), whereas what needs to be examined are disparities of a more general character. As we will see later, growth in inequality generally spreads through a population from above and ends up squeezing the middle class, something that this indicator is not well-suited to representing. But this goal has the merit at least of having been formulated, above all in view of the political battles it provoked: at the United Nations, the United States and China initially resisted integrating it among the SDGs, for ideological reasons, whereas the Scandinavian countries, France, and Brazil argued for its inclusion.[6]

What explains the fact that reducing inequalities within countries, which was not even on the international political agenda (or indeed on national agendas) ten years ago, is now the cornerstone of sustainable development policies? In order to understand how inequalities and sustainable development are related, we must consider a large number of studies in economics, political science, epidemiology, and ecology that over the past several decades have made a compelling case that high levels of economic inequality endanger democracy, sicken society, harm the economy, and tend to damage the environment.

Democracy under Stress

THE IDEAL OF SOCIAL JUSTICE

Achieving social justice is the avowed aim of most modern states, democratic or otherwise. The first article of the French constitution establishes a republic in which collective solidarity is held up as a means of guaranteeing the equality of social rights. The declared purpose of the Indian constitution is similar; so too that of the Algerian, Russian, and Chinese constitutions. The list goes on. In the modern world, the pursuit of social justice is the rule rather than the exception.[7]

This does not mean, of course, that states—whether dictatorships or parliamentary democracies—do everything in their power to attain the goal that they have set for themselves. We will see in the next section that inequalities are widening almost everywhere in the world. But the inability of states to guarantee social justice and to narrow, if not actually eliminate, economic inequality undermines their very legitimacy. Authoritarian regimes can allow themselves, through repressive measures or by falsifying public information, the luxury of disregarding their solemn undertakings, but democracies cannot do this for very long.

SOCIOECONOMIC INEQUALITY AND ELECTORAL EXTREMISM

Donald Trump's victory in the 2016 American presidential election and the vote in Great Britain earlier that year to leave the European Union have caused much ink to be spilled, and surely there is much more yet to be said. What was the determining factor of these results? Some authors maintain that they are explained on objective socioeconomic grounds (notably, increases in inequality); others hold that the principal cause is a subjective feeling among certain ethnic groups of a loss of power in the face of rising levels of immigration.[8]

Recent studies go some ways to reconciling the two interpretations.[9] Studying the sources of the Brexit vote, the German economist Thiemo Fetzer found that support for the pro-Brexit, far-right UKIP party was stronger where austerity cuts had been more severe, everything else being equal. In other words, where disposable incomes and social services were hit harder, the temptation to blame foreigners was greater. Focusing on several Western countries, researchers at McKinsey, the American management consulting firm, found that persons whose income has stagnated in the past few decades are more inclined to have a negative opinion of immigration and a positive opinion of nationalist parties. To be sure, correlation is not causality, nor can a vote for the extreme right or a rejection of the "system" justifiably be reduced to economic factors alone; the crisis of meaning that has shaken Western societies in the postmodern age (loss of faith in the ideal of progress, weakening of familiar cultural and religious allegiances, and so on) goes deeper than that. But it seems obvious that the levels of inequality observed in the United States and the United Kingdom have helped to demobilize the historical voting base of self-styled progressive parties and also to create a favorable atmosphere for the spread of xenophobic feeling.[10]

INEQUALITY AND THE POLARIZATION OF POLITICAL LIFE

Inequalities also harm the proper functioning of the electoral and parliamentary machinery of democratic regimes. The French economist Julia Cagé has demonstrated that the amount of public funding spent on elections is sharply declining in Western democracies (such as the United States or Italy),[11] with the result that political parties are obliged to rely increasingly on private donations. The basic problem with the private financing of electoral campaigns is that those who have more wealth can invest more, and those who invest more have a greater chance of winning, as the data reveal. In this way, the modern democratic ideal of "one person, one vote" comes to be replaced by another: "one dollar, one vote." This situation is also liable to perpetuate existing political and economic inequalities.

High rates of inequality also tend to polarize political competition. In a prescient work first published in 2006, the American political scientists Nolan McCarty, Keith Poole, and Howard Rosenthal argued that the greater inequalities are, the more polarized political life becomes and the more difficult it is to reduce them.[12] They studied the record of congressional roll-call votes on various issues over recent decades as well as the results of opinion surveys during this period in order to construct a "political polarization index." The reliability of this measure is limited by the fact that it requires the use of complex algorithms that compromise methodological transparency. But it nonetheless has the advantage of making it possible to trace the development of secular trends. The authors show that political polarization evolved in tandem with income inequality during the course of the twentieth century, the two falling together between 1913 and 1957 and then rising dramatically from the mid-1970s onward.

For this phenomenon—"the dance of ideology," in their phrase— McCarty, Poole, and Rosenthal offer the following explanation: with growing income inequality, the wealthiest have fewer and fewer objective reasons to support policies aimed at reducing it (for they will be taxed at ever higher rates); and this in turn has led to a rightward shift in the policy positions of the Republican Party. They also examine the role of immigration since the 1970s, observing that the increase in the number of poor citizens with low rates of political participation, and of resident aliens lacking the right to vote, means that there is bound to be less political support for redistribution than against it.

Furthermore, the polarization of economic and social debate exerts a dampening effect on bipartisan legislation: the greater the degree of polarization, the fewer laws that are passed. As the French economist Éloi Laurent has pointed out, the polarization of political debate prevents the formation of "transpartisan" electoral coalitions on issues of environmental and health policy.[13]

Societies Sickened by Inequality

It is now well established that the level of income is one of the principal determinants of life expectancy. The World Health Organization has set forth ten "solid facts" that, taken together, explain why the poorest tend to be in worse health than the average. The list includes exposure to substandard living conditions at a young age, lifelong stress, dangerous work environments, restricted social interaction, and poor diet.[14] Note that we are talking here not of inequalities in themselves but of poverty. On this view, then, there is not necessarily any need to reduce differences in income between individuals, only to address the problem of poverty itself. A landmark study by the British epidemiologists Richard Wilkinson and Kate Pickett has shown, however, that differences in income concentration do in fact matter.[15]

In 2009, when their book first appeared, it was commonly accepted in the English-speaking world that the richest had no *objective* interest in reducing income inequality. Wilkinson and Pickett stood this opinion on its head: not only does inequality raise a moral question, it has practical implications for all members of society, rich and poor alike, altruistic or not. Among wealthy countries, they point out, the most egalitarian ones score the highest with regard to social well-being. Levels of equality are strongly correlated with levels of physical and mental health, education, economic security, and social mobility. Wilkinson and Pickett argue that a causal mechanism is at work here: these results depend on the *relative* social position of individuals. With respect to health and educational outcomes, this is explained in particular by the stress generated in inegalitarian societies, at all levels of the social scale. As a consequence, reducing poverty without reducing inequalities will not be enough to address the health and social problems observed in inegalitarian societies.

Their argument is illustrated by a simple graph (Figure 1.1) representing the performance of various rich countries with regard to social health (a composite statistic that measures physical and mental health with reference to levels of infant mortality, adolescent pregnancy, education, economic security, and social mobility) as a function of the level of economic inequality. Here we find a clear correlation between equality and the variations in national performance measured by this index. In Japan, for example, where the level of inequality is low, health and social well-being scores are the highest among OECD member countries. Conversely, when one compares average income and social health performance, no correlation is observed. In rich countries, then, health depends more on income differentials than on average income.

Evidently these results must be interpreted with caution. We need to keep in mind once more that correlation is not causality, as students in introductory statistics courses are regularly told. By itself, the graph

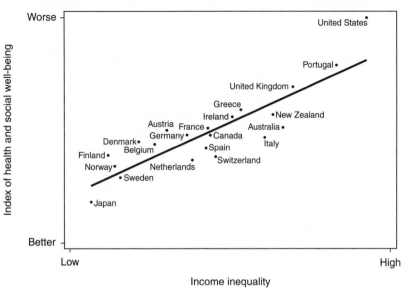

Figure 1.1. Income inequality and social well-being. Disposable income inequality measured in terms of the Gini coefficient. In Japan, where the level of inequality is low, health and social well-being scores are the highest among OECD countries. Data for 2005. *Sources and series:* Wilkinson and Pickett (2010); www.lucaschancel.info/hup.

does not allow us to assert that income inequality is responsible for all these evils, or that reducing inequality will automatically eradicate them. Other factors may indeed be involved: on the one hand, a more or less great cultural tolerance for inequality in some countries; on the other, a more or less favorable environment for the development of certain illnesses. In that case a good score would not necessarily be due to a low level of inequality, but to deeper cultural, political, or geographic factors. Another possibility is that the state of a society's health is the cause, rather than the consequence, of the observed level of economic inequality.[16] But Wilkinson and Pickett seek to go beyond mere correlation by advancing a theory that explains the causal relation between inequalities and health problems. Their argument suffers from one disadvantage in particular, namely, that it analyzes data for the most part on the scale of countries or regions. Individualized data (measures of inequality and health at the level of a single person, not of a whole country or group of countries) would provide a firmer basis for analysis. For the moment, the few studies that do make use of individual-level data do not suffice to decide the matter one way or the other.[17] Even so, Wilkinson and Pickett offer a cogent explanation of the connection between inequality and public health that deserves to be taken very seriously.

INEQUALITY, HEALTH, AND ANXIETY

How does economic inequality affect the physical and mental health of individuals? Wilkinson and Pickett insist on the cardinal importance of public services. The high quality of such services in the least inegalitarian societies, especially in connection with health care, has positive effects that are almost universally felt. This became evident in the context of the COVID-19 pandemic, especially in the United States and countries without universal health care. Deprived of affordable health care, the poorest segments of society cannot be properly treated, placing them as well as society as a whole at high risk. Inequality in access to basic services such as health care affects all social groups: this is the idea that underlay the introduction of national health insurance schemes in the United Kingdom and France right after World War II. But Wilkinson and Pickett also lay emphasis on a less obvious factor: stress. Not all stress is bad, of course; up to a certain point, some kinds may even be beneficial. But chronic stress, beginning in early childhood, may lastingly weaken an individual's health.

Epidemiological studies have shown that stress predisposes to a variety of pathologies, including obesity, diabetes, hypertension, and cardiovascular disease. It weakens the immune system and reduces fertility, causes digestive problems, impairs cognitive function, and heightens the risk of depression.[18] A massive recent European study on the life course of eighteen thousand British people born in 1958 shows that childhood stress and traumatizing events at an early age measurably affect the probability of developing breast and uterine cancers later in life.[19]

Stress may also be generated by what psychologists call "social evaluation threats," which are all the stronger as the rate of inequality increases in a society. Injustice at a systemic level generates stress in persons at the bottom of the social ladder, but also, according to Wilkinson and Pickett, in persons above them, particularly those who are resolved to maintain themselves and their families at the top of the ladder. What makes stress a matter of special concern for public policy, in other words, is the fact that, through it, inequalities act on the health of society as a whole.

INEQUALITY, EDUCATION, AND STATUS ANXIETY

Inequality also affects educational outcomes and the ability of students to learn. Total household income largely determines a child's school performances, the level of study reached, and future earnings. The economists Emmanuel Saez and Raj Chetty have shown that, in the United States, the higher the parents' income, the likelier it is that their children will go to college: fewer than 30 percent of children from the poorest 10 percent of families go on to higher education, as opposed to roughly 90 percent from the wealthiest 10 percent.[20] These results are explained in part by the exorbitant tuition fees charged by American institutions of higher learning, which the scholarship system, contrary to what its defenders claim, has not in any substantial way succeeded in democratizing. But beyond the financial question, research also shows how social stress influences the outcomes of relatively disadvantaged children, which is to say independently of a certain revenue threshold. In other words, it is not enough to guarantee access to primary education for the poorest children; if social inequality persists outside schools, educational inequality will be lasting as well.

A study conducted in India by the World Bank economists Karla Hoff and Priyanka Pandey yielded striking results.[21] It showed that there is a clear link between pupils having to publicly declare their caste before trying to solve a math problem and their ability to solve the problem. Prima facie, there should be no relation between belonging to one or another caste and mastering this type of exercise: the data clearly show that students from wealthy and socially favored families are not stronger in mathematics than others. The researchers observed the behavior of more than six hundred boys between the ages of eleven and twelve, half upper caste and half lower caste, in villages throughout the country. Although discrimination on this basis has officially been abolished in India, it is nonetheless very much a reality.

The pupils were asked first to solve simple geometric problems, without having to indicate their caste or knowing the caste of the others. No difference in results was observed as a function of the caste to which they belonged. Next they were required to state their name and caste before attempting to solve the problems. Here a very clear drop was observed in the performances of those born into a lower social class; among those of higher social status, by contrast, there was no effect. These results show that being reminded that one is at the bottom of the social ladder and knowing that one is perceived as having inferior status strongly influences cognitive ability.

Similar findings have been obtained in the United States in tests on white and African American students conducted by Claude Steele and Joshua Aronson at Stanford University.[22] They asked a group of young people to solve simple problems without telling them anything about the point of the exercise. No differences related to skin color were observed. But when it was made clear to the students that the tests were meant to evaluate their abilities, the results for the African Americans sharply dropped. Studies of this sort call attention to the role played by stress due to status anxiety, or what Steele and Aronson call *stereotype threat*. A similar mechanism also explains some of the inequalities observed between men and women.

The human propensity to be inhibited or stimulated by one's *relative* social position is a product in part of biological evolution; indeed, similar behaviors are found in our closest animal cousins. Two American neurochemists, Michael Raleigh and Michael McGuire, studied the biochemical mechanisms associated with social status among vervets, a species of African monkey.[23] Male vervets live in groups composed of a dominant male and dominated males. Raleigh and McGuire were interested in comparing levels of serotonin. In these groups of monkeys, the dominant male has a higher serotonin level than the other males. This higher value is explained partly by his status within the group: once isolated from the others, whom he has been accustomed to dominate, his serotonin level falls; at the same time, the serotonin level of the formerly dominated male who takes his place rises. When the isolated leader is reintroduced to the group and resumes his dominant status, his serotonin level rises; conversely, the level of the one who took his place, now again one of the dominated, falls.

What explains these variations? The fact of being placed in a dominant position can positively stimulate the organism; being placed in a dominated position has the opposite effect. This mechanism helps to stabilize social interactions by awarding a physiological bonus to the leader. This in turn makes groups of monkeys potentially more capable of defending themselves against external aggression, thus offering them an evolutionary advantage.

In humans, similar mechanisms may help to perpetuate social inequalities, notably by stimulating dominant individuals and by limiting the development of mental capacities that would lead to educational success among the most disadvantaged young people. Neuropsychological studies have made it possible to more precisely specify the link between status-related stress and cognitive performance: a supportive, reassuring environment in which one feels at ease encourages the release of dopamine, a hormone associated with the brain's reward system, which also favors memory, attention, and the ability to solve problems.[24] Such an environment also causes the secretion of serotonin and adrenaline, which help us to be more efficient; conversely, when the organism is subject to prolonged stress, it is flooded with cortisol, which inhibits mental abilities and memory.

These biological mechanisms interact with purely social strategies (the structure and financing of educational systems, for example), many of which are designed to serve the interests of the upper classes. One thinks in this connection particularly of the work of Pierre Bourdieu on the function of schools and universities in reproducing social inequalities.[25]

Inequality and Economic Performance

We have just seen that inequalities influence the health of the population as a whole and affect the level of education of a given society. Let us now turn to the relationship between inequality and economic growth, or, more broadly, between inequality and a healthy economy.

Let us begin by recalling a theory I mentioned earlier, which for several decades strongly influenced thinking about this relationship. It was illustrated by the famous Kuznets curve, plotted in 1955 by the Belarusian American economist Simon Kuznets, a future Nobel laureate, who argued that income inequality rises during the initial stages of a country's development and then flattens out before finally falling, at least in the case of the United States, the United Kingdom, and Germany between the end of the nineteenth century and the middle of the twentieth.[26]

The explanation Kuznets gave for this pattern is that when a society industrializes, some will benefit from the strong growth of the industrial sector and others will not—hence the rise in inequality in the initial phases of a country's development. This is the first part of the bell-shaped curve. But as industry absorbs more and more workers from traditional sectors (agriculture, artisanal trades, and so on), inequalities gradually diminish. Kuznets maintained that the industrial sector had an incentive to treat low-income workers relatively well, because otherwise they were apt to organize and demand wage increases. A society's overall level of income therefore increases with industrialization, and inequalities within this sector tend to diminish over time. Nevertheless, as Piketty has shown, Kuznets's argument suffers from major weaknesses. The observed reduction of inequalities, far from being automatic, was largely an accidental consequence of the two world wars (which destroyed many of the factories and much of the industrial equipment owned by the rentier class), the Great Depression (which unleashed a wave of bankruptcies that substantially reduced, and sometimes wiped out, the capital of the richest), and of inflation (which ate away at the value of inherited and accumulated wealth, reaching record heights between 1915 and 1950 after a century of almost uninterrupted price stability).[27]

The decline, and then the stagnation, of inequality was also a consequence of the exceptional political circumstances of the postwar period, a historic moment of consensus regarding the need for social cohesion and solidarity after the terrible agonies that had torn apart European society. It was during the immediate postwar period that the rate of taxation on upper incomes reached its highest level in the West. Data collected since Kuznets published his results indicate a rise in inequality in almost all countries beginning in the late 1970s—further confirmation that the dynamic of inequality is in no way a tranquil or mechanical economic process; it is instead the result of social and political forces whose effects are more often violent than not.

It should be kept in mind, too, that the question Kuznets posed has nothing to do with the impact of inequality on growth, but precisely the reverse: what effect do different stages in a country's development have on the level of inequality within that country? Let us now take a look, then, at this aspect of the relationship between inequality and growth.

CAN INEQUALITY BE GOOD?

The impact of economic inequality on growth has long been a subject of controversy. The economist Arthur Okun argued that income differentials encourage entrepreneurs to innovate and workers to work harder. On this view, reducing inequality entails a net loss for the economy—hence the metaphor of the leaky bucket: when money is redistributed from the rich to the poor by the government, part of it is lost in the form of administrative costs. From this Okun concluded, "We can't have our cake of market efficiency and share it equally."[28] Many other economists have suggested that there might be a positive relation between inequality and growth: Nicholas Kaldor, for example, held that an inegalitarian distribution of incomes increases the level of savings in an economy.[29] This in turn adds to the amount of investment that is permitted by savings and that, from the macroeconomic point of view, shapes the rate of a country's economic growth.[30]

The idea that there might be trade-offs of this kind between efficiency and equality, and that the purpose of political debate is to discover the proper balance between these two objectives, is by no means absurd on its face. Nevertheless it is increasingly clear that reducing inequality does not have the negative effect on growth that has long been assumed. International Monetary Fund (IMF) economists have recently shown that, in almost all cases, policies aimed at reducing inequality have not adversely affected growth over the past three decades—invalidating the leaky-bucket thesis.[31] A number of other recent studies have arrived at the same conclusion.[32] Let us briefly consider several examples involving labor productivity.

INEQUALITY REDUCES LABOR PRODUCTIVITY

Recent research in behavioral economics, conducted in countries that are culturally very different, supports the conclusion that income inequality affects workers' motivation. In an experiment designed to measure the effect of wage differentials on effort in the workplace, the economist Alain Cohn and his colleagues studied a Swiss firm that hired employees on a temporary basis to sell promotional cards permitting entry to certain nightclubs and bars on specific dates.[33]

In the first phase of the experiment, the employees, who worked in teams of two, were paid the same hourly wage. In the second phase, the wages of some team members were randomly cut. The idea was to artificially create wage discrepancies and then to observe the effects of these changes on the sale of cards. Whether this type of experiment is ethically defensible may be doubted, but I shall not enter into that debate here.

In the first phase, during which all employees were paid the same wage, each team member sold on average twenty-two cards a day. In the second phase, the teams were divided into three groups. Teams in the first group, which served as a control group, fared best: the hourly wage was not reduced for either member. Teams in the second group were the least fortunate: both members' wages were cut by 25 percent. In the third group, the wage of only one member was cut, again by 25 percent; the other's remained unchanged. The employees were told that their wage cuts were ordered by the firm's management, but nothing more.

The results of the experiment were unequivocal. Sales made by the first group (stable wages for both team members) increased by roughly 10 percent in the second phase: having the benefit of experience, they knew which techniques worked and which ones did not. Sales made by the second group (wage cuts for both members) fell by 15 percent, not a negligible figure. Sales made by the penalized members of teams in the third group (whose wages fell in relation to those of their partners) were more than 30 percent lower than those made by the first group, whereas the performance of their fortunate colleagues (whose wages were unchanged) was identical to that of the employees in the control group.

From this it may be concluded that inequalities can cause productivity losses among disfavored workers that outweigh the gains produced among workers who are favored by these inequalities. Very comparable results have been obtained by a similar experiment in India, suggesting that this aversion to inequality extends across cultures.[34]

Another study of the same type was made by economists at the University of California, Berkeley, showing that job satisfaction is partly determined by relative wages (rather than the level of pay).[35]

They too found that earning more than the baseline wage for a given job does not increase workers' satisfaction, whereas earning less has a negative effect, prompting underpaid workers to change employers. We are therefore far from Okun's hypothetical world in which inequality stimulates innovation and encourages workers to work harder.

These results will seem self-evident to many readers. Studies of this kind in behavioral economics are vulnerable to the objection that they prove the obvious or else set out to disprove what noneconomists, at least, consider to be implausible. But many unrealistic assumptions (that individuals are all rational, for example, or that they do not care about inequalities, or that they are purely selfish) nonetheless continue to enjoy considerable influence in the world of economic research and among some decision makers. It is therefore important to conduct exactly this type of empirical research at the intersection of psychology and economics, in order to probe the limits of what economic models can reasonably assume.

INEQUALITY AND MACROECONOMIC PRODUCTIVITY

We saw earlier that inequality is associated with lower levels of education and health among the poorest members of society (and with worsening health among the richest as well). This evidently poses an ethical problem, but from an economic point of view it is also counterproductive: the economy of a country with declining educational performance is one in which young people have a harder time entering the labor market, in which workers are less capable of doing their jobs, and in which there is less innovation. The Italian economist Federico Cingano, in a study of OECD countries, has argued that educational inequality produced by differences in income accounts for most of the impact of economic inequality on growth.[36]

Joseph Stiglitz, another Nobel laureate in economics, concurs. But he goes farther, pointing out that this situation is self-perpetuating: differences in wealth favor control by elites over policy making, particularly with regard to the balance between public and private investment.[37] In an inegalitarian society, those whose fortunes enable them to exercise political power will tend to favor investment that serves their short-term interests, to the detriment of society as a whole in the medium term, not only in respect of education, but also of health, adequate public transportation, and so on. A decline in socially useful investment, Stiglitz maintains, reduces the level of economic growth by preventing individuals from realizing their full potential.

Inequality and Financial Crises

Another argument has been developed by Raghuram Rajan, a former chief economist and director of research at the IMF, who holds that unequal distribution of wealth in the United States was not the least of the factors that led to the financial crisis of 2008, which in turn aggravated these same inequalities.[38] Where the benefits of economic growth are unequally distributed, low-wage workers see their standard of living stagnate, while the richest see their incomes increase. In order to maintain aggregate consumption (one of the engines of year-on-year growth) at a constant level in the years leading up to the crisis, low-income persons were encouraged to take on more debt in the belief that real estate values would continue to rise. At the top end of the pyramid, the wealthiest borrowed money on the financial markets that they could no longer very easily spend (additional consumption begins to approach a limit once one has a yacht and three homes), thus further expanding the real-estate bubble and intensifying the speculative frenzy that fed on it. But the ability of low-income households to repay their mortgages being what it was (which is to say very low), the boom years could not last forever.

This model is nonetheless not generalizable to all economic crises. Even in the case of the subprime crisis one could argue that an event of this kind still might have occurred even with a much lower level of inequality, as long as the American financial system was managed—as it continues to be today—primarily for the benefit of those at the top. But it must be admitted that the combination of stagnating incomes and credit-financed consumption at the bottom was explosive, and may well be explosive in the future.

Environmental Degradation

The quality of the environment is no less threatened by inequalities of various kinds. There are a number of reasons for this, involving both economic factors (inequality influences consumption habits) and political factors (inequality makes it more difficult to win legislative approval for environmental policies and then to put them into effect). Several recent studies have concluded from this that reducing economic inequality therefore must be good for the environment. We will see later, in Part Three, that this does not go without saying. There are different ways of reducing inequalities, and not all of them have the same value from the environmental point of view. To begin with, however, we must understand how economic inequality can worsen pollution.

KEEPING UP WITH THE JONESES

Because we are social animals, our behaviors are often influenced by the propensity to compare ourselves to others. The desire to do as well as one's neighbors—keeping up with the Joneses, as the expression has it—and, if possible, to do still better than one's neighbors, is deep-seated in human nature.

The need to compare ourselves to others influences in turn our habits of consumption. When we buy clothes, a car, or a home, we do it in part to tell others—not only our peers, but those to whose condition we aspire (which is to say those whose good opinion matters to us)—that we enjoy a certain standard of living. Gustave Flaubert, through the character of Madame Bovary, who found to her dismay that purchasing power did not bring the happiness and social prominence she longed for, well understood that the act of consuming is much less "objective" than it seems, that it fulfills a set of psychological and social needs. Considering the United States today, the Israeli economist Ori Heffetz has shown that the greater one's income, the larger the share of disposable income that is devoted to buying socially visible goods.[39]

The workings of this mechanism were penetratingly analyzed more than a century ago by the American economic sociologist Thorstein Veblen.[40] In *The Theory of the Leisure Class*, Veblen argued that each social class seeks to imitate the consumption habits of the one above it in order to distance itself from the one beneath it. This idea of the invidious nature of consumption had been anticipated by Adam Smith's notion of a human need for recognition; later it was to be echoed by the English economist Fred Hirsch's concept of positional competition, and by the French sociologist and philosopher Jean Baudrillard's concept of differentiation.[41] Marketing specialists are very familiar with this effect. Apple, to name only one of a nearly endless number of examples, blithely makes use of it in advertising its iPhones: by purchasing the latest model, consumers buy more than a new and improved (according to the ads) bundle of applications—they buy themselves social status.

For Veblen, the more inegalitarian the society, the more its members are led to consume visible goods in order to distinguish themselves from some and to identify themselves with others. The economists Samuel Bowles and Yongjin Park have shown more recently that the most inegalitarian societies are also ones in which people spend the most time working in the course of a year.[42] According to data from the early 1990s, if the same level of inequality existed in the United States as in Sweden, Americans would work 10 percent fewer hours annually, not a trivial number. Bowles and Park propose a "Veblen effect" to explain this: in an inegalitarian context, one seeks to work more in order to be in a position to reproduce the lifestyle of those whom one envies.

What bearing does this phenomenon have on the fate of the environment? It is harmful for the planet because rising levels of consumption brought about by a desire to copy the lifestyles of the rich and famous lead to an increase in pollution. To the extent that these lifestyles are ecologically less sustainable than those of everyone else, in other words, our predicament will become more dire. As we will see in Part Two, incomes and pollution levels are closely related. The contest for social distinction is played out in large part through the accumulation of cars with big engines that produce more pollution, large houses that use more energy and eat up more land, expensive vacations halfway around the world that increase carbon emissions, and so on, all of which magnify the human impact on the environment. The very wealthy do, of course, also consume more goods and services having a smaller carbon footprint (privately exhibiting a work of art uses less energy than driving a fancy car), but at the same time they own more cars and live in larger houses than the rest of society.

POISONING THE POLITICAL WELL

We saw earlier that economic inequality tends to polarize political debate. In the United States, the growing inequality that marked the Reagan years inaugurated a dark period for environmental policy.[43] The preceding decade, by contrast, when partisan disagreements over economic justice were less pronounced, had begun with the creation of the Environmental Protection Agency, in 1970.

The radicalization of political debate accompanying the election of Donald Trump is the most recent and the most extreme illustration of this dynamic. In June 2017, fulfilling a campaign promise, Trump announced America's withdrawal from the Paris Agreement on climate change. Under the terms of the treaty, this executive order cannot take effect before November 4, 2020, one day after the next presidential election—which leaves a faint glimmer of hope, if the Democrats manage to regain the White House. Trump said it was necessary to leave the Paris Agreement because it harmed American workers and threatened the country's energy security. Whatever his real motives may be, it is interesting that he should have resorted to an argument from social justice (the protection of workers) to justify his decision. But is it a sound argument? It is clear that climate protection requires a gradual abandonment of coal, and therefore a reassignment of workers in the coal industry. Coal miners represent only 0.05 percent of the American workforce. In principle, then, targeted compensatory measures could be designed whose cost would be relatively painless for the rest of the population to absorb. It is true that in pro-Trump swing states with a long-established coal industry, the number employed is not inconsiderable (2.5 percent of the workforce in West Virginia); it is still larger if to this figure are added the families of these workers, who stand to be materially affected in the event that mining activity were to be severely curtailed. But here again it is altogether possible to engineer a gradual transition, by protecting people rather than a particular type of employment or polluting sector. I shall come back to this topic in Part Three.

As we will also see in the following sections, low-income American workers are and will be the first victims of the consequences of climate change in their country. Yet in the context of wage stagnation at the lower end of the scale in the United States, and considering the inability of progressive political voices since then to make a convincing argument in favor of the social benefits of environmental policies, Trump's dramatic break with international norms no doubt boosted his polling numbers in mining states, to the detriment of the environment and the health of people everywhere.

This is a familiar tactic, of course, and by no means a monopoly of the political UFO that is the forty-fifth president of the United States. Take an example in France: ten years before the yellow vests movement (which I will discuss later in the book), the center-right government tried to implement a carbon tax. A part of the opposition on the left took issue with what it saw as an "antisocial" measure that would disproportionately affect low-income workers and rural households more than others. These segments of the population rely on automobiles in order to get to work and to do daily errands—unlike the so-called bourgeois bohemians of the major cities, who take public transportation during the week and fill up their cars with gas only when they go away on weekends. Poor families also lack the financial means to adapt to higher energy costs in their homes.

The claim that a carbon tax would be inequitable aroused widespread public dismay and helped to sink the project, in large part because many opponents of the tax who hardly cared about the issue of equity were pleased to be able to take cover behind this argument.[44] Here again we see that otherwise sensible environmental measures are apt to be thwarted by the discontent to which socioeconomic disparities give rise, not only in France but in many other countries as well.

Conversely, Scandinavian countries such as Sweden and Norway—pioneers in the matter of taxation on pollution from CO_2 emissions that also enjoy low levels of social inequality—benefited from a political culture characterized by interparty consensus in order to implement environmental legislation in the early 1990s. More generally, research conducted during this period by the future Nobel laureate Elinor Ostrom demonstrated the importance of a high degree of social cohesion in managing environmental resources within small communities.[45]

Of forty-two recent empirical studies on the relation between inequalities and environmental quality, fifteen show that inequalities harm the quality of the environment, nine show the opposite, seven arrive at results that depend on the level of income (inequalities have no environmental impact in poor countries, but they do have an impact in rich countries), and eleven find no statistical relationship between these two dimensions. What are we to conclude from this? That caution is warranted: inequality tends to make environmental protection more difficult, but reducing inequality by no means automatically improves the environment. More research in this area is needed and the good news is that this line of inquiry is now attracting considerable interest.[46]

It is nonetheless plain that an unprecedented consensus among a variety of different actors (environmental activists, elected officials, business leaders, nongovernmental organizations, international institutions) has grown up around the necessity of reducing economic inequality. This consensus is explained in part by the fact that there is now increasing evidence that economic inequality, however objectionable it may be from an ethical point of view, also affects all aspects of sustainable development: democracy, health, the economy, the environment. But the consensus is also the result of new information about inequalities that is now being published and widely consulted.

2

Trends and Drivers of Economic Inequality

THERE IS A BROAD CONSENSUS that inequalities have risen in recent decades after a historical decline in rich countries and in large emerging countries. But what exactly are the trajectories and orders of magnitude that need to be taken into account? How are published data to be interpreted? It needs to be kept in mind that measuring inequality is not only a scientific undertaking, but also an administrative and political one. Presently observable trends depend on how one chooses to look at them, which is to say on which segment of the population is selected for analysis (does one look at the top 1 percent, or the bottom 50 percent, or some other group?) and on the quality of the data that can be marshaled for this purpose.

The Historical Evolution of Inequality

The Gini coefficient is a composite measure of inequality having a value of zero when there is perfect equality and a value of one (or 100 percent) when there is perfect inequality, that is, when only one person owns all available resources. Let us begin by considering Gini coefficients of income inequality for different countries, which since the beginning of the twentieth century have never fallen below 20 percent and never exceeded 68 percent.

Changes in the coefficient's value over the past thirty years reveal a sustained rise in income inequality in almost all developed countries, with the most pronounced increases occurring in the United States and in Scandinavia, a region that had a low level of inequality at the beginning of the 1980s. A few countries have managed to resist this trend: Belgium, France, and the Netherlands have done better than most of their European neighbors—even if income and wealth differentials have widened in these same countries over the past three decades.

The Gini coefficient has one advantage by comparison with other measures: its panoramic view. The Gini coefficient tells us about changes in inequality in society as a whole—or, more precisely, it yields a composite picture of inequality in the distribution of income in a given society. It has the disadvantage, however, of failing to capture deepening inequality at the bottom and the top of the social pyramid. Moreover, it can mask significant developments in the middle, notably the inability of middle-class incomes in recent decades to keep pace with the gains registered by other segments of society.

Consider the following example. The Gini coefficient of world income inequality was 65 percent in 1980, rising to 68 percent in 2003 and falling back to 65 percent today. It is therefore tempting to speak of stagnation in global inequality during this period. Figure 2.1 nonetheless plainly discloses an important dynamic at work behind this apparent stability: those in the top 10 percent, whose incomes rose dramatically over the period by comparison with the world middle class, are pulling away from it, whereas those in the lower half are catching up with this same middle class. The Gini coefficient gives no insight into this state of affairs.

The limitations of the Gini coefficient are compounded by limitations inherent in the data that international bodies currently use to measure inequalities of personal income and accumulated wealth. In trying to piece together historical patterns, they rely for the most part upon door-to-door interviews, sometimes also using surveys conducted by telephone or via the internet. These are very useful when

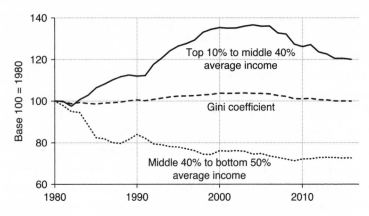

Figure 2.1. Global income inequality dynamics, 1980–2016. Distribution of per adult pretax national income, measured at purchasing power parity. In 2016, the global pretax income Gini coefficient was equal to its 1980 value. The gap between the incomes of the top 10 percent and incomes of the middle 40 percent had increased by 20 percent in 2016 as compared to 1980. *Sources and series:* www.lucaschancel.info/hup.

no other source of information is available, but they have a number of drawbacks. Generalizing about the financial situation of very wealthy people is not easy, for though they are relatively few in number they are often reluctant to be interviewed and have a tendency, when they are willing to respond to questions at all, to underestimate their income and their wealth. Additionally, it is often difficult to compare the results of such inquiries over time and across countries, because the methodologies and definitions of income and wealth employed vary according to period and place.

In order to provide more reliable and comparable inequality data, a group of economists created WID.world, an open-access database of historical series on inequalities of income and accumulated wealth throughout the world. WID.world differs from other tools for measuring inequalities by its use of tax records, systematically analyzed and combined with other sources of information (including surveys and published national accounts). This approach carries on the tradition of Kuznets's work, mentioned earlier, and over the course of the past fifteen years it has been put back on the research agenda in economics by Thomas Piketty, Anthony Atkinson, Emmanuel Saez, and Facundo Alvaredo.[1]

In 2011, these economists created the World Top Incomes Database (WTID) and invited the collaboration of Gabriel Zucman, a specialist in wealth inequalities and tax avoidance. I was fortunate enough to be asked to join the project in 2015 and am now its codirector. In 2017 we renamed it the World Inequality Database (WID.world), for its purpose had been enlarged in the interval to incorporate series on inequalities in inherited wealth, to cover the distribution of all incomes (not just the highest incomes), to take greater account of developing countries, and to broaden the scope of our inquiry to include gender inequality and, as far as possible, environmental injustice. WID.world brings together more than a hundred researchers on five continents working in more than a hundred countries.

Comparing the data collected by WID.world with standard data from household surveys, it becomes clear that current measures of inequality underestimate inequality at the top end of the income scale. According to official household surveys, the top 1 percent of Europeans earn on average €18,000 per month. Using more precise data for top earners shows that this figure is actually €28,000 per month, more than 50 percent higher.[2] Similar conclusions can be drawn for other rich countries—and the discrepancy is even greater in the case of emerging countries. It is therefore always important to ask which index is assumed when one is talking about inequalities, and what type of data is being analyzed.

THE EXPLOSION OF TOP INCOMES

Any measure of inequality rests on a certain view of justice in a given society, represented by a social welfare function. In order to be able to compare different countries using the Gini coefficient, one must make a series of normative choices associated with the mathematical properties of this index; taken together, these choices constitute the social welfare function. The adequacy of these choices has long been questioned, however, beginning with the British economist Anthony Atkinson, who almost fifty years ago argued that the social welfare function implied by the Gini coefficient does not reflect commonly accepted criteria of justice.[3]

A simple and persuasive way of following the evolution of inequalities is to observe the share of incomes (or of wealth) allocated to different income groups—for example, the richest 10 percent (or 1 percent), the 40 percent in the middle, or the poorest 50 percent. For the purpose of studying changes in the share of the pie enjoyed by these different groups, the right sort of social welfare function is more illuminating than the Gini coefficient. It is generally agreed that a society in which the share of income captured by the richest (the top 10 percent, or the top 1 percent) grows ever larger, compressing the share of poorer groups (the bottom 50 percent, or the middle 40 percent), is increasingly inegalitarian. But it is not enough to analyze the movement of "explicit" indicators; reliable data are needed as well. Precise information on the evolution of top incomes and inherited wealth can be obtained by consulting tax return data. Unlike surveys, these records indicate how much is officially declared by individuals to the authorities. The very wealthy can underestimate their income only at the risk of committing fraud, which to some extent limits inaccurate filings.[4] Notwithstanding all the mechanisms of tax evasion and optimization used by the fraudulent rich (which WID.world tries to incorporate as fully as possible, particularly in the wake of the Panama Papers), the important thing is that these data are more trustworthy than the data yielded by methods that are still standard among international organizations today. Let us take a closer look at what can be learned from the data archived in the WID.world database, which, as I say, combines information from tax returns, surveys, national accounts, and, whenever possible, information concerning tax evasion, in a transparent and systematic manner.

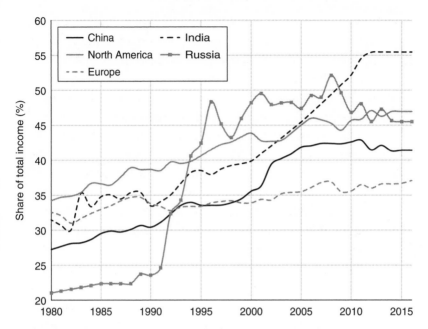

Figure 2.2. Top decile share of national income in China, Europe, India, Russia, North America, 1980–2016. Distribution of national income per adult, before taxes but after social transfers (pension and unemployment benefits). North America refers to US-Canada. In 1991, the wealthiest 10 percent captured 25 percent of total income in Russia; by 1996, this share had increased to about 48 percent. *Sources and series:* www .lucaschancel.info/hup.

Inequalities have increased in most countries since the 1970s, but not at the same rate (Figure 2.2).[5] Take the most extreme case, Russia. In 1980, it was the most egalitarian of the countries (groups of countries in the case of Europe and North America) considered here, with the share of income held by the richest 10 percent accounting for slightly more than a fifth of the national total. This means that average per capita income among the richest ten percent was twice that of the average for the population as a whole. In the space of scarcely more than fifteen years, Russia became the most inegalitarian: the share of the top 10 percent exceeded 45 percent, which is to say that per capita income within this group was four and a half times higher than the national average. The rise in the North American trajectory, by contrast, though clearly more gradual, was nonetheless impressive. In the United States and Canada, the wealthiest 10 percent accounted for less than 35 percent of total income in 1980, but more than 45 percent in 2016. In India as well, starting from a relatively low level in 1980 (the top 10 percent captured about 30 percent), income inequality reached an extremely high level—55 percent—thirty-five years later. In China, it widened over the period, but flattened out from 2005 onward. In Europe, income inequalities increased clearly less rapidly than in the rest of the world (the top 10 percent rising from 33 percent to 37 percent in the interval).

Even in rich countries, grouped together in Figure 2.2 in two blocs (North America and Europe), significant differences can be observed. The rise in inequality is more pronounced in English-speaking countries (Figure 2.3a) than in the major countries of continental Europe (Figure 2.3b). The share of income earned by the top 1 percent in the English-speaking countries fell from a range of roughly 10–20 percent in the 1910s to 5–10 percent in 1980, then climbed back to 10–20 percent today. The United States constitutes an extreme case in this connection: there the share of the top 1 percent was just below 20 percent in 1915, fell to almost 10 percent in 1980, and rebounded to 20 percent after 2005, whereas the share of national income of the bottom 50 percent has fallen sharply in recent decades, from about 20 percent in 1980 to about 10 percent today. In France and Germany the share of the top 1 percent dropped from about 20 percent at the beginning of the century to 7–10 percent in 1980, rising thereafter to about 10–13 percent today. Conversely, the share of the bottom 50 percent shrank markedly less in these countries than in the United States: in France it was fairly stable between 1980 and 2016, and in Germany during the same period it dropped from 23 percent to 17 percent.

Figures 2.3a and 2.3b illustrate an important point: in a long historical perspective, it becomes apparent that levels of inequality in the late 1970s and the early 1980s, for a very large part of the world's pop-

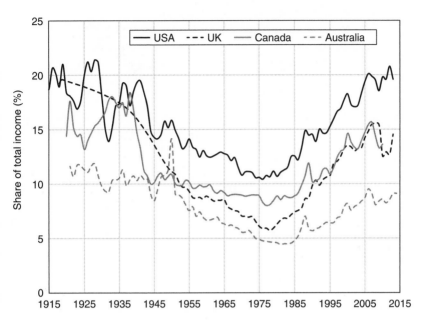

Figure 2.3a. Top centile share of national income in Australia, Canada, United Kingdom, United States, 1915–2014. Distribution of national income per adult or tax household before taxes on personal income and net worth but after social transfers (pension and unemployment benefits). *Sources and series:* www.lucaschancel.info/hup.

ulation, were relatively low. The economic liberalization of the early 1980s can now be seen to have marked the end of a leveling off of inequalities in income and accumulated wealth that began during the interwar period under very disparate political and economic regimes: mixed economies in Europe and the United States, Communism in Russia (and after 1949 in China), highly regulated economies in India and elsewhere. Following the economic historian Karl Polyani, we may say that this period was characterized by a more or less violent "embedding" of markets.[6]

What was going on in other parts of the world? Until now I have omitted to discuss Africa, Brazil, and the Middle East, all of which have displayed relatively stable levels of inequality in recent decades, but also

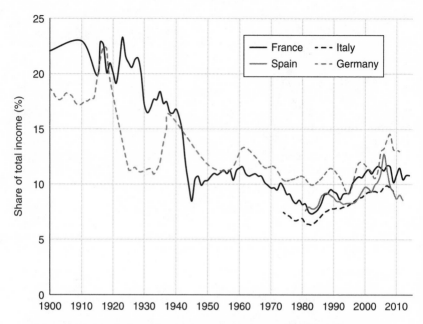

Figure 2.3b. Top centile share of national income in continental Europe, 1900–2014. Distribution of national income per adult or tax household before taxes on personal income and net worth but after social transfers (pension and unemployment benefits). In France, in 1900, the wealthiest 1 percent received about 22 percent of total income. *Sources and series:* www.lucaschancel.info/hup.

staggering levels of income concentration: the share of the top 10 percent in these regions is equal to or greater than 55 percent of total national income. Countries there did not undergo the historical phase of reduced inequality that developed countries experienced in the first half of the twentieth century. Today they constitute an upper bound, in effect, on the level of inequality that human beings seem to be capable of generating. The question arises whether societies that have known low levels of inequality in the past are necessarily doomed to revert to a condition of extreme inequality later. I shall come back to the divergences among countries observed since 1980 in due course. For the moment it is enough to say that they show that the sudden reemergence of economic inequality is in no way foreordained. Ultimately, it is a matter of political choice.

THE DECLINE OF PUBLIC WEALTH AND THE EXPLOSION OF PRIVATE WEALTH

Another major economic fact of recent decades, often overlooked, is the decline of public wealth at a time when private wealth has increased considerably. The wealth of a country, or its capital (the two words can be used interchangeably for our purposes), comprises the whole of the country's nonfinancial assets (infrastructure, real estate, mineral deposits, and so on) and financial assets (stock shares, foreign exchange reserves, and so on) excluding debts incurred to the rest of the world.[7] By definition, then, national wealth has a private component and a public component.

Each of these components may be expressed as a percentage of national income (Figure 2.4). The United Kingdom, for example, possessed private wealth equivalent to 300 percent of national income in 1970. This means that its people could then have stopped working for three years and continued to enjoy the same standard of living as before. After three years, however, they would have had to go back to work, for they would no longer have had any assets left to sell.

The value of public wealth, for its part, fell from about 70 percent of national income in rich countries at the end of the 1970s to zero percent of national income today—indeed, lower than zero percent in the United States and the United Kingdom, the result of transferring public wealth to the private sphere through the privatization of government functions and of an increase in public indebtedness. Let us pause for a moment to consider what net negative public wealth implies. Historically, it is exceptional and generally not long-lasting. A negative public wealth position means that if a country wants to pay its debts, selling all its assets (hospitals, roads, schools, financial holdings, and so on) will not be enough. Furthermore, the country's citizens would then have to pay rent to the new owners of the entire stock

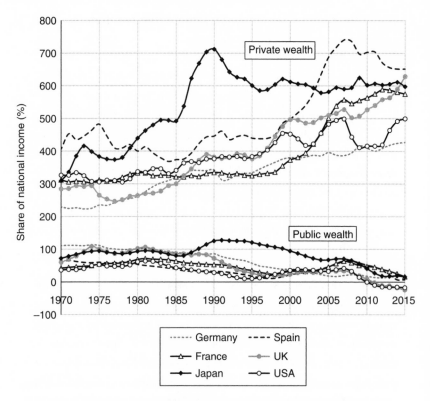

Figure 2.4. Wealth of nations, poverty of states, 1970–2015. Wealth refers to the sum of all financial and nonfinancial assets held by private or public actors, net of their debts. In 1970, private capital in the United Kingdom was about 300 percent of national income; in 2015, it was above 600 percent. *Sources and series:* www.lucaschancel.info/hup.

of assets—which is to say every school, road, hospital, or other existing form of infrastructure—since absolutely all the country's wealth will have been privatized. This is, in many regards, an undesirable situation.

Conversely, private wealth has doubled over the past few decades, rising from 300 percent of national income to more than 600 percent today in the rich countries. The bursting of real-estate bubbles (in Japan and Spain) and the financial crisis of 2008 seem not to have had any effect whatever in slowing this trend.

A dramatic increase in private wealth, accompanied by a steady decrease in public wealth, has important consequences for inequalities among individuals. On the one hand, low levels of public wealth make it more difficult to carry out policies for reducing such inequalities (through investment in education and health, for example, or in programs designed to promote ecological transition, as we shall see a bit later). On the other hand, the increase in private wealth is associated with growing inequalities among individuals: wealth distribution is more concentrated than income distribution over time since the greater one's wealth, the more rapid its accumulation.

WEALTH INEQUALITY OUTPACES
INCOME INEQUALITY

The combination of a rise in income inequality and a rise in private wealth as a share of national wealth has led to a historic rise in wealth inequality in many parts of the world since the 1980s (Figure 2.5), though once again at variable rates. The share of wealth of the richest 1 percent of Americans was between 45 and 50 percent in the second decade of the twentieth century, then fell slightly below 25 percent in the 1970s and subsequently rose to about 40 percent today. In France and the United Kingdom this share was clearly greater in the early twentieth century: almost 60 percent in France and 70 percent across the Channel. In the United States, during the 1930s, the New Deal was partly based on a rejection of the prewar European model, which was much more inegalitarian than American society in respect of wealth. Since then, however, the positions have been reversed. In France and the United Kingdom, the share of wealth owned by the richest 1 percent fell to about 15 percent in the 1970s, thereafter climbing back to about 20 percent. In China, the adoption of free-market principles and the privatization of a part of the economy have had the effect of considerably increasing wealth inequalities among individuals: twenty-five years ago the richest 1 percent held roughly 15 percent of the nation's wealth, compared to about 30 percent today.

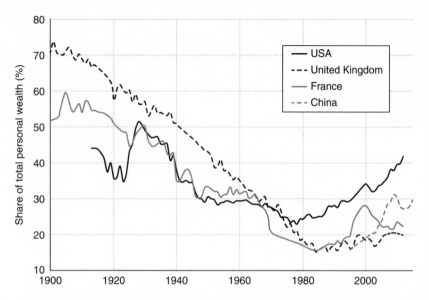

Figure 2.5. Top centile share of national wealth in China, France, United Kingdom, United States, 1900–2015. Distribution of net personal wealth per adult; for China, France, and the United States, the wealth of couples is equally shared. In 2015, the wealthiest 1 percent in China held 30 percent of total national wealth. *Sources and series:* www.lucaschancel .info/hup.

We have less information concerning wealth than income—and still less in the case of developing and emerging countries—but the various sources available to us all indicate a rise in inequality in recent years.[8] The twenty-first century, from the point of view both of wealth and income, is on track to match the extreme levels of inequality observed in the nineteenth century, where this has not already occurred (as in the case of income concentration in the United States). What are the causes of this historic rise?

The Principal Causes of Economic Inequality

Rather than enter here into a detailed analysis of the causes of economic inequality, I shall limit myself to presenting the principal elements in order to clarify what is at issue.[9] A basic understanding of the main factors contributing to economic inequality (and of the remedies that have been proposed) will be needed in order to follow the argument I go on to develop about the relation between economic inequality and the environment.

TECHNOLOGICAL INNOVATION

Some economists consider that inequality in earned income is the consequence of a race between technological change and education.[10] On this view, the innovations that have shaken the world over the last thirty years have led to a greater demand for highly educated workers. As long as the level of education among workers who are less well trained does not increase, the dynamics of supply and demand ensure that the more highly educated will earn more. The more highly educated therefore stand to benefit more than others from the productivity gains associated with technological innovation.[11]

This explanation has the virtue of emphasizing the importance of taking into account educational qualifications, and the scientific and technological context in which a society evolves, in trying to measure the extent of inequality in that society. The lack of professional training among the unemployed and the increasing number of young people who drop out of school help to explain the discrepancies in earned income observed in the United States and in many European countries. But this way of approaching the problem does not account for growing inequality at the top of the social ladder, both within and across countries.

On the one hand, new technologies have penetrated all rich countries to more or less the same degree over the past thirty years, but income inequalities have followed strikingly different trajectories. On the other hand, among the richest 10 percent one finds individuals with very similar educational qualifications and professional backgrounds whose incomes have varied significantly in recent decades. The evolution of the incomes of the wealthiest 1 percent therefore cannot be explained as a result of superior training and experience by comparison with the 9 percent below them.[12]

Nevertheless this does not mean that more broad-based investment in education is not an important element of policies designed to reduce economic inequality, particularly at the bottom of the ladder—quite the contrary. Nor does it mean that technological innovations will not accelerate the growth of inequality in the future if they are not subject to stringent regulatory review. But the race between innovation and education cannot by itself account for the explosion of inequality at the apex of the social pyramid that has been observed in a number of countries since the 1980s.

In a provocative article titled "Defending the One Percent," the American economist Gregory Mankiw goes further.[13] The wealthiest, he maintains, are not only better educated but intrinsically more talented than the rest. What then explains the fact that inequalities have clearly increased over the past thirty years in some countries but not in others? Was the talent of the wealthiest "intrinsically" multiplied in relation to the rest of the population in English-speaking countries and not elsewhere? The chief executives of the largest German companies earn two times less than their American counterparts, yet it seems difficult to argue in light of the performance of companies in the two countries that German executives are less talented than American executives.[14] Here the argument from intrinsic talent is used to justify a certain state of affairs without making a serious attempt to understand the underlying dynamics.

TRADE GLOBALIZATION

Another explanation that is often put forward holds that the increase in inequality is due to the effects of trade globalization, which is to say the growing proportion of world production that crosses international boundaries.[15] The opening up of commerce through the General Agreement on Tariffs and Trade (GATT) in 1947, and subsequently in the framework of the World Trade Organization (WTO) in the 1990s, put low-skilled workers in developed countries in competition with those in emerging and developing countries.

The increase in inequality in developed countries was predicted and explained more than seventy years ago by one of the most important results of international trade theory, the Stolper-Samuelson theorem.[16] Trade liberalization, the theorem states, leads to increased demand for unskilled workers in the countries of the South (where they are supposed to be "abundant") and a relatively greater demand for skilled workers in the countries of the North (for the same reason), which leads in turn to an increase in inequality in rich countries and a corresponding reduction of inequality in poor countries.[17]

Subsequently it became necessary to explain why Stolper and Samuelson's model had been contradicted by events, since trade did not take place to the extent forecast between countries richly endowed with skilled labor in the North and countries richly endowed with unskilled labor in the South, but predominantly between countries in the North instead. Moreover, most economists long continued to insist that the negative trade effects predicted by the theorem were limited, if not in fact nonexistent, in industrialized countries, chiefly because trade liberalization enabled low-wage workers in these countries to purchase less expensive goods, which therefore strengthened their purchasing power.

Not quite fifteen years after the publication of his influential 1994 book on international trade, Paul Krugman did an about-face, saying that he had not taken into account all the relevant information in his earlier work (for which, by a twist of fate, he was shortly thereafter to be awarded the Nobel Prize).[18] This work, he now claimed, needed to be reinterpreted in the light of new data on the evolution of inequality.[19] Owing to the strong market penetration of goods from emerging countries since the 1990s, trade globalization could now be seen to be a good candidate for explaining the rise in inequality in the industrialized world. As for new technologies, however, although the rich countries all opened up to international trade at about the same rate and in the same proportions, inequality did not follow the same trajectory everywhere. The rates of penetration of Chinese products within the European Union and in the United States are not too different, whereas the rising levels of inequality in these areas have been far from uniform. On balance, then, trade globalization probably explains at least part of the general tendency for economic inequality to increase, particularly through international competition among low-wage workers, but it does not explain the considerable divergence in trajectories between countries.

FINANCIAL GLOBALIZATION

The other aspect of globalization, having to do with financial flows, makes it possible to explain in a rather convincing manner the rise in inequality at the very top end of the income distribution scale. The opening up of capital markets can have several effects. On the one hand, liberalization increases both their size and their yields, thanks to the economies of scale it permits (many transaction costs disappear as the volume of business increases, so the returns on invested capital are greater), and the gains are redistributed to a minority of top managers in the financial sector, in the form of higher salaries and related benefits (stock options and so forth), sometimes amounting to staggering rates of compensation.[20] On the other hand, financial liberalization increases the returns on inherited wealth. Empirically one observes that the higher the initial inheritance, the greater the returns thirty years later—hence the snowball effect of concentrated wealth and income from invested capital.[21]

A recent study by the Swedish economists Julia Tanndal and Daniel Waldenström reveals a link between the increase in inequality at the top end of the scale and deregulation in Japan and the United Kingdom.[22] In these countries deregulation occurred in fits and starts, making it easier to identify its effects (when it occurs gradually the effects are obscured by the variable and simultaneous action of other factors). Tanndal and Waldenström found that financial liberalization accounts for an increase of roughly 15 percent in the share of income earned by the richest 1 percent in the decade following liberalization. This is by no means a trivial increment, but once again it does not explain everything: even without financial liberalization, the research suggests, the share of the top 1 percent would have increased by 45 percent. Plainly, other powerful forces must also be at work.

Before examining these other forces, let us pause for a moment to note parenthetically an interesting and, to say the least, surprising interpretation of the origins of financial liberalization advanced by Rawi Abdelal, an authority on international management at Harvard Business School. In spite of its name, Abdelal argues, the so-called Washington Consensus on financial liberalization was first devised in France under a leftist president, François Mitterrand, whose economic advisors saw loosening capital flows as a way to hasten the formation of a patrimonial (or propertied) middle class.[23]

As we have just seen, the growth of financial wealth over the past several decades has mainly benefited those at the summit of the pyramid. The middle class, by contrast, has gained more from home ownership than from financial assets, enough to limit its losses by comparison with the richest people in Europe. Because middle-class wealth, unlike that of the upper class, consists chiefly of residential property, the rise in real-estate prices, especially in the United Kingdom and in France, has favored the middle class at the expense of the working class, very few of whose members own their own homes. Whatever the policy motivations of financial liberalization may have been, its effect has been to aggravate inequalities within countries rather than to reduce them.

WEAKENING OF THE SOCIAL STATE

The weakening of the social state over the past thirty years (with regard to tax policies, workers' protections, public services, and so on) is a decisive factor in explaining the increase in inequalities of income and wealth.[24]

In this connection it is necessary to distinguish between mechanisms of *predistribution,* such as a minimum wage, which make it possible to narrow income inequality generated by markets, and mechanisms of *redistribution,* which correct for unjust market allocations.[25] The former type of mechanism has been weakened whenever inequality has grown. In this regard the case of the minimum hourly wage mandated by federal law in the United States is instructive. In 1968, when the minimum federal wage reached its peak ($11.80 per hour in current dollars), it was 60 percent higher than the federal statutory minimum wage fifty years later ($7.25 per hour).[26] There are several reasons for this, notably the erosion of the relative bargaining power of labor unions. In France, by contrast, a rich country that has recorded relatively small increases in inequalities, the minimum hourly wage before tax has steadily risen over the past thirty years, from €2.5 in 1968 to €9.9 in 2018, allowing for inflation. A minimum wage was also recently established in Germany and in the United Kingdom, again following a different path than in the United States.

International Monetary Fund (IMF) economists Florence Jaumotte and Carolina Osorio Buitron have made a more general analysis of this situation, studying the evolution of inequalities and rates of unionization in twenty industrialized countries since 1980.[27] They found that the decline in union membership accounted for 40 percent of the increase in the income share of the richest 10 percent, and was associated with less redistribution.

Redistributive mechanisms play a substantial role as well. In the 1990s, such mechanisms made it possible to reduce inequalities by half in Organisation for Economic Co-operation and Development (OECD) countries; today, reductions are only 30 percent on average.[28] To put it another way, current inequalities are 40 percent higher than they would have been if the level of redistribution were the same as it was thirty years ago, other things being equal. Among these mechanisms, it is necessary to distinguish between social transfers (or benefits)—payments made by governments to individuals and households, whether in cash (housing assistance, for example) or in kind (free transportation, for example)—and taxation (which may be progressive or regressive).

Today, social transfers tend to do more than taxes to reduce inequalities in disposable income in most industrialized countries.[29] It needs to be kept in mind that the progressivity of such transfers diminished between the late 1990s and the end of the first decade of the present century. With regard to taxation, particularly of income, the marginal tax rates (rates levied on earned income beyond a certain threshold) to which the wealthiest individuals are subject have clearly decreased over the past thirty years, falling on average from about 70 percent to 40 percent in OECD countries. In the United States during the period 1950–1980 they were on average about 80 percent, reaching a peak of 91 percent in 1963. Moreover, the rates of other taxes levied on the wealthiest—taxes on dividends and corporate earnings—have very clearly fallen since the early 1980s, from 75 percent to 48 percent for dividends and from 42 percent to 25 percent for corporate earnings in OECD countries.[30] Comparing national histories for this period, one observes that inequalities increased markedly where top marginal tax rates were significantly reduced (United States and United Kingdom), moderately where these rates were not significantly reduced (Germany and France), and negligibly where they were unchanged (as in Switzerland, where the share of national wealth accruing to the wealthiest 1 percent has remained high since the 1960s).[31]

There is a strongly negative relationship between the top marginal tax rate and the share of national wealth captured by the wealthiest 1 percent. Thomas Piketty, Emmanuel Saez, and Stefanie Stantcheva have shown that when the marginal tax rate falls by 1 percent, the share of the top 1 percent increases by 0.5 percent.[32] The OECD arrived at similar conclusions, illustrated in Figure 2.6.[33]

Note that here we are speaking of a correlation between pretax income and tax rates; naturally it would be still stronger if one were to look at income *after* taxes. But how could the marginal tax rates of the

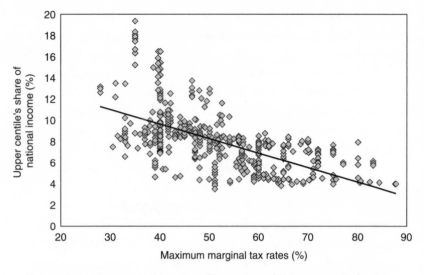

Figure 2.6. Maximum marginal tax rates and income inequalities, 1975–2012. Each point represents the wealthiest 1 percent share of a country's total income as a function of its maximum marginal tax rate at a given time. The downward sloping line plainly shows that the lower the marginal rate, the higher the share of national income. *Sources and series:* OECD (2014); www.lucaschancel.info/hup.

wealthiest individuals affect their income *before* taxes? Piketty, Saez, and Stantcheva show that the principal mechanism operating in this case is leverage: the richest have a greater interest in negotiating pay increases when the top tax rates are low. Extremely high rates can also have a deterrent effect, by reducing incentives for innovation and hard work on the part of the wealthiest, potentially with the result of depressing the overall level of economic activity and boosting unemployment. And yet Piketty and his coauthors calculate that top tax rates could be as high as 80 percent without anyone being worse off—apart from the richest of the rich.

THE GROWING POLITICAL POWER OF THE WEALTHIEST

At another level of analysis, some authors emphasize an increase in the power of owners of capital over workers and society in general. On this view, the rise in inequalities over the past thirty years is explained by the fact that capitalists prevailed in their struggle against workers following the collapse of the Communist countermodel, with the consequence that social protections have been weakened, the minimum wage lowered in real terms, and so on. The investor Warren Buffett made headlines more than ten years ago when he declared: "There's class warfare, all right, but it's my class, the rich class, that's making war, and we're winning."[34]

More recently, the American political scientists Martin Gilens and Benjamin Page attracted notice when they published a study showing that American economic elites have much greater power than the average citizen to translate their ideas into policy.[35] Their findings acquired still greater resonance with the election of Donald Trump and the passage of a GOP tax reform bill benefitting the richest Americans and their heirs (which meant that for the first time in recent history, billionaires pay lower taxes than the working class).[36]

Using quantitative data and survey information, Gilens and Page demonstrate that economic elites and lobbies representing business interests are clearly able to influence public policy, whereas average citizens have little impact or none at all. This echoes the work of the French economist Julia Cagé, discussed in Chapter 1.

This political perspective is wholly compatible with the other explanations for the increase in inequality we have looked at. The weakening of the social state and the intensification of financial and trade globalization are a result of political decisions due in large part to the growing political power of owners of capital over the rest of society. They are mainly a result, in other words, of political decisions that can be counteracted.

THE ROLE OF ENERGY

At this point anyone reading a book with a title such as mine may well feel justified in asking what role the present ecological crisis, and energy in particular, plays in the increase of inequalities since 1980—and all the more when one considers that the oil shocks of the 1970s were accompanied by a historic rebound of inequalities and accumulated wealth in the industrialized countries.

Let us begin by noting that inequality levels throughout the world and within certain regions are closely linked to the distribution of natural resources (particularly oil) and to property rights to these resources. As we have seen, the principal hydrocarbon-producing region, the Middle East, is one of the wealthiest and most inegalitarian parts of the world, a consequence of its vast oil revenues being administered by a very small number of high-ranking officials for the benefit of a tiny elite.

Nevertheless fluctuations in fossil fuel prices—rather than the scarcity of these resources, which is entirely relative—cannot account for the full impact of the trends I described earlier. Higher energy costs probably did play a role (albeit a limited one) in increasing unemployment and inequality in certain oil-importing countries, through a rise in production costs, passed on in the form of lower wages and sustained by policies and legislation lowering labor costs.[37] The increase in oil prices has also weighed heavily on household budgets. The economist Robert Kaufmann and his colleagues have also shown that many low-income American households at the beginning of the subprime crisis had to choose between repaying their home loan and putting gas (the price of which had more than tripled in ten years) in the car— in order to go to work and meet their mortgage payments. Households burdened by high energy bills were among the first no longer to be able to repay loans.[38] Without being the principal cause, the cost of energy nonetheless contributes to high mortgage delinquency rates in certain countries. I shall examine this relationship more fully in Part Two.

The Need for a Concerted Political Response

The increase in economic inequality is due to many factors, then, and it would be pointless to insist on the overriding importance of only one. While the tendency for inequality to grow is common to most countries, specifically national features can be observed in a great many cases. We must therefore be careful not to overgeneralize. The process of financial and trade globalization that began in the 1980s, as well as technological innovation in a context of unequal access to education and professional training, go some ways to explaining the general tendency to increase, but they do not readily account for the variations observed among developed countries. Taking into consideration the slashing of budgets for social programs, through lower taxes for the wealthy and policies aimed at shrinking the social safety net for the poor, makes it possible to better understand the diversity of outcomes.

Some authors have used three letters as a shorthand in summarizing the debate over the causes of economic inequalities: P (for policies), O (for openness), and T (for technology). Most economists agree about the combined effect of these three major sets of factors, but some (the so-called POT group) put policies before technology (reckoned to be paramount by members of the TOP group).[39] How the letters are arranged is not unimportant: whichever explanation of the rise in inequalities is preferred will determine the order of priority for implementing policy reforms (involving taxation, investment in education, new rules concerning globalization in trade and finance, and so forth)—assuming, as everyone does, that merely going forward as we have done until now is not an alternative. Policy making is a question of deciding between different options, even if some combination of them can always be contemplated. One of the main items on the political agenda in the years to come will be formulating a persuasive and detailed account of the causes and consequences of the increase in inequalities.

The distinction between policies, openness (another name for globalization), and technology is nonetheless liable to give rise to confusion. Political choices themselves help to determine the openness of a country to the rest of the world (or the way in which a country opens up) as well as the type of technological and social innovations that are made, as the Italian American economist Mariana Mazzucato has powerfully demonstrated.[40] The increase in inequalities results from the choice not only of fiscal, social, and educational policies, but also of trade and industrial policies. It goes without saying that predicting the evolution of trends is fraught with uncertainty. But in the absence of a concerted attempt to reduce these inequalities, there is every reason to believe that they will continue to increase.

On a global scale, the dynamic of income inequality is governed by two main forces. The first is the compression of inequalities between rich countries and emerging countries. The standard of living of the average Chinese worker, for example, is gradually catching up with the standard of living of the average North American worker, and this tends to reduce inequalities among individuals across countries. The other force is the growth of inequalities within countries, which affects a majority of the world's population. In a recent study, my coauthors and I observed that the second force has been predominant since 1980.[41] In other words, despite the rising standards of living in emerging countries by comparison with rich countries, the share of the world's income possessed by the top 1 percent has grown since the 1980s as a consequence of the pronounced increase in inequality within countries. We also show that if the trends observed within countries are not reversed, global inequalities will continue to increase, and this even with strong growth in emerging countries in Asia, Africa, and Latin America.

It is possible that the assumption that inequality will continue to increase within countries, prolonging a pattern documented since 1980, will not be borne out by events. Other trajectories may supervene. But without concerted political action, our forecast is likelier than not.

In Part One we have seen that a consensus has already emerged within international organizations such as the United Nations, the IMF, and the OECD that economic inequality constitutes a real problem for societies everywhere. Until now only the objectives of reducing differences in average incomes between countries and eradicating poverty have been on the agenda of the international community. Including the reduction of economic inequality as one of the United Nations's sustainable development goals is a sign that a paradigm shift is now taking place.

This new consensus is fortified by research in economics, political science, epidemiology, and ecology on the links between economic inequality and the various aspects of sustainable development. Recent studies show that unless inequalities are reduced it will be extremely difficult to improve democratic governance and effectively address urgent social, economic, and environmental problems. These findings are all the more disturbing as the increase of inequalities within countries since the 1980s affects a majority of the world's population.

Even so, the outlook is not altogether bleak. The increase in inequalities is largely the result of public policy choices—in favor of diminished tax progressivity, weakened social protections for workers, reduced investment in worker training, and financial deregulation—whose effects can be offset by other and better policies. There is nothing inevitable about the course of present trends.

We must now examine the complex relationship between economic inequalities and another form of injustice that lies at the heart of unsustainable development: environmental inequalities.

PART TWO

The Vicious Circle of Environmental and Social Inequalities

3

Unequal Access to Environmental Resources

THE ENVIRONMENTAL CRISIS we are presently experiencing—a warming climate; biodiversity loss; polluted air, soil, and water—is usually described as an injustice committed by all those who are alive today in bequeathing an ill-fated future to all those who will come after them.[1] This is partly true, particularly as far as the climate is concerned, since it takes several decades for CO_2 emissions to have a warming effect on the atmosphere, sometimes with irreversible consequences for ecosystems. But this way of looking at the problem misses a piece of it, for several reasons. First, we do not all have the same access to natural resources, any more than we are all equally exposed to environmental risk: a catastrophe does not affect everyone with the same intensity, for some are better able to protect themselves against it than others. Second, not everyone bears the same degree of responsibility. Third, because the crisis is unfolding in real time, those who are responsible for polluting the air and for contaminating soils and water are contemporaries of those who are the first to be harmed.

The environmental crisis therefore forces us to examine how natural resources are shared and who bears responsibility for degrading them, considering not only successive generations but also members of the same generation. To understand what is at issue, it will be useful to distinguish between five forms of environmental inequality:

- unequal access to natural resources
- unequal exposure to the risks of environmental disturbance
- unequal responsibility for the degradation of natural resources
- unequal exposure to the effects of environmental protection policies
- unequal say in decisions concerning the management of natural resources.[2]

Taken together, these topics raise two key questions: How do environmental inequalities manifest themselves? How do they interact with economic inequalities?

In this chapter I take up the matter of access to resources, and then, in Chapter 4, the matter of exposure to risks and the assignment of responsibility. The last two forms of environmental inequality I address in Part Three.

Energy Inequalities

Energy is a natural resource that may take many forms: a barrel of oil, a log of wood, wind and flowing water, heat in a room, the warming rays of the sun. The polymorphous character of this resource allows us to feed ourselves, to move around, and to keep ourselves warm. Access to energy is therefore a basic condition of human existence.

THE CENTRAL ROLE OF ENERGY
IN ECONOMIC DEVELOPMENT

To begin with, access to a sufficient quantity of energy is necessary to guarantee a decent standard of living. In developing countries, having electricity means not only that it will be possible to refrigerate foods and therefore reduce the risks of food poisoning, but also that lighting will be available for working, studying, and recreation indoors or after nightfall. Moreover, access to a modern source of energy for heating (such as gas) frees girls and women from the hard work of gathering wood that is their lot in many parts of the world, thus helping to reduce gender inequality.

Evidently the question is not limited to developing countries. Energy insecurity has real consequences for health, employment, and socialization in rich countries as well. Insufficient access to heating fuel increases the chance of contracting respiratory illnesses due to the spread of mold and mildew in the absence of heat.[3] Moreover, gasoline is very often what economists call a nonsubstitutable good, which is to say that it cannot (or cannot easily) be replaced. When its price goes up, decisions having potentially grave consequences need to be made: we saw earlier that in the United States, in 2007, many households were obliged to choose between paying for gas in order to go to work and making their home loan payments.[4] In both cases the result has proved to be dramatic. For all these reasons, differential access to energy recommends itself as a point of departure for studying environmental inequalities.

LEVELS OF UNEQUAL ACCESS TO ENERGY

In order to properly understand the orders of magnitude involved, let us go very far back into the past, seven thousand years or so. The planet then was still largely populated by hunter-gatherers whose diet consisted of plants, fruits, game, and fish, every day consuming a certain number of calories. The human body has changed relatively little over the intervening seven millennia: then, as today, the daily requirement seems to have been about 2,000 kilocalories.[5] One may check this by looking at the values indicated on food packaging: a can of cola provides us with 140 kilocalories—equivalent, we are told, to 7 percent of the daily energy required by someone who engages in only light physical activity (approximately 2,000 kilocalories). The math looks about right.

This amount of energy may be expressed by another unit, one that we see on our electricity bills: the kilowatt hour (kWh). Two thousand kilocalories is equivalent to 2.3 kWh, roughly the daily energy consumption of a freezer. In a hunter-gatherer society, the basic diet would have provided pretty much everyone with the same amount of energy, and therefore daily per capita consumption may be supposed to have been 2.3 kWh. Adding to this the energy contained in the wood that was burned in cooking food (about 0.5 kWh per person per day), we arrive at a total figure of 3.0 kWh.

Inequalities of energy consumption, like economic inequalities, increased as human populations became settled, specialized, and stratified. Some individuals—those who tilled the earth without the aid of domesticated animals, for example, producing just enough to feed themselves—continued to consume 3 kWh per day; others, who were able to harness beasts or make use of machines, or exploit the energy of fellow human beings in order to satisfy their needs, managed to considerably exceed this threshold of survival. Ancient Egypt is an extreme case: a pharaoh who mobilized ten thousand skilled and unskilled workers as well as a thousand pack animals in order to build a pyramid indirectly consumed more than 40,000 kWh per day.[6]

Back to the twenty-first century: who consumes what kinds of energy and how much? In order to have a complete picture of what each of us consumes, we must take into account not only the energy needed to feed ourselves, heat our homes, and go from place to place, but also so-called indirect (or gray) energy—the materials and labor required to build our homes and manufacture our personal computers, the electricity a cinema uses to project a film, the auxiliary heating in our doctors' offices, and so on. The calculation is complicated by the fact that indirect energy consumption often occurs abroad (the manufacture of mobile phones is a familiar example). Taking all these things into consideration is not easy, but it can be done by comparing international trade data (concerning which industrial sectors buy what from which other sectors and in which countries) with data about energy consumption by sectors and individuals.[7]

Doing this, we discover that on average a North American today consumes about 300 kWh per day—roughly 100 times more energy than a hunter-gatherer seven thousand years ago, and more than a hundred times less than an Egyptian pharaoh in the third millennium BCE. A European consumes about two times less than a North American; in France, for example, 150 kWh per day is needed to maintain a normal standard of living. An Indian consumes more than twenty times less than a North American, on the order of 13 kWh per day.

But these average values conceal substantial disparities among individuals. Homogeneous data between countries over time about direct and indirect energy consumption are sparse, but research is rapidly advancing. For France (Figure 3.1), I have tried to address this problem in collaboration with Prabodh Pourouchottamin, Carine Barbier, and Michel Colombier.[8] We found that someone belonging to

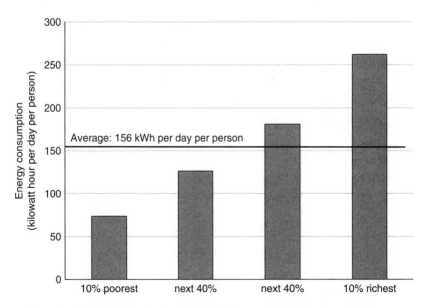

Figure 3.1. Energy consumption inequalities in France, 2004. The poorest 10 percent consume 70 kWh per person per day. *Sources and series:* www.lucaschancel.info/hup.

the bottom 10 percent in respect of income consumes about 70 kWh per day, not quite half of the average figure. Someone belonging to the top 10 percent consumes more than 260 kWh per day, or about 70 percent more than the average and 3.6 times what a member of the lowest decile consumes.

I shall come back later to the connection between energy consumption and income. For the moment let me simply observe that income is a good indicator of total energy expenditures, even if the gap between the richest and the poorest seems at first sight greater for income than for energy consumption. Why? There are two reasons. On the one hand, because energy is a vitally important good, low-income individuals are obliged to devote a certain part of their budget to it, whatever their exact financial position may be. On the other hand, beyond a certain threshold of income, energy consumption continues to increase as individual income increases, though at a slower rate: the wealthiest do not spend all their income on gas to keep their cars running and their jets flying; they also purchase goods and services that have a relatively small energy content (works of art, for example). This has the notable consequence that inequalities in energy consumption are smaller than income inequalities. In France, for example, the richest 10 percent account for 34 percent of total income and 17 percent of total energy consumption.

Let us compare these results with those from India (Figure 3.2).[9] We saw earlier that levels of energy consumption there are much lower than in the United States or France. At the bottom of the social scale, the poorest 10 percent (some 120 million people) require about 6 kWh per person per day to satisfy basic needs. This is only 2 kWh more than prehistoric hunter-gatherers—another way of measuring the extreme poverty in which tens of millions in India still live today. The richest 10 percent, by contrast, consume about 32 kWh per person per day.

The low level of energy consumption by the top 10 percent in India by comparison with the corresponding figures for wealthy countries may come as a surprise. It does not mean, however, that the energy

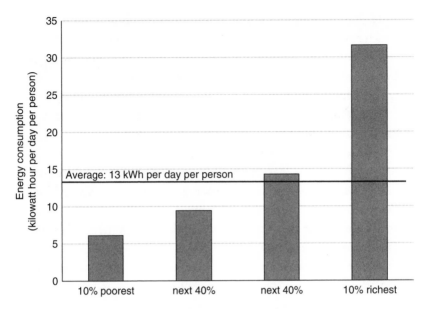

Figure 3.2. Energy consumption inequalities in India, 2011. The poorest 10 percent consume 6 kWh per person per day. *Sources and series:* www.lucaschancel.info/hup.

consumption levels of the very wealthiest Indians are not comparable to those of the wealthiest individuals in Western countries. If we look more closely at the top 10 percent, zooming in on the upper extremities of this bracket (top 1 percent or even somewhat larger segments), we find that energy is consumed at rates much closer to those in Europe and North America. But in relation to the immense size of the country's population (numbering more than 1.3 billion), those who enjoy Western standards of living are still *relatively* few.

Unequal Access to Potable Water

Beyond energy inequalities, access to many environmental resources exhibits a strong socioeconomic gradient. In the latest installment of the dystopian *Mad Max* saga, *Fury Road* (2015), the protagonists clash in a fantastic struggle for access not only to gasoline, but also to water, which has become scarce. The world's remaining supply of fresh water is controlled by a despotic tyrant who keeps his people in submission by regulating the operation of sluice gates. Notwithstanding its somewhat ridiculous plot, the film has rightly been praised for drawing attention to one of the foremost problems of the twenty-first century: unequal access to potable water.

According to the World Health Organization, an adult requires a minimum of twenty liters (5.3 gallons) of water per day in order to satisfy the basic needs of drinking, cooking, and personal hygiene.[10] The minimum required to satisfy all elementary needs (also taking into account water for household sanitation, washing clothes, and so on) pushes the daily usage up to about seventy liters per person. Adding in water usage for leisure purposes (such as gardening or, for those who can afford the luxury, maintaining a hot tub) may bring the total to more than 200 liters per person per day.

To a greater degree in the case of water than of energy, direct consumption of the sort I have just described represents only the tip of the iceberg by comparison with indirect consumption, which is to say the amount of water involved in producing the goods and services that we consume. With regard to indirect water usage, the quantities are quite considerable—typically thirty times greater than direct usage (as opposed to four times for indirect energy usage versus direct usage).

A major component of indirect water usage is food production. It takes 1,200 liters of water to produce only one kilogram (2.2 pounds) of wheat, for example, and more than 13,000 liters to produce a kilogram of beef. Water consumption inequalities among countries therefore depend in large part on differences in standards of living and dietary habits: a North American consumes on average about 7,000 liters of water per day, as against 3,400 for a Briton, 2,600 for a South African, and 1,900 for a Chinese.[11]

On the global scale, there is enough fresh water to meet the current needs of humanity. The fundamental problem concerning water is its unequal distribution. Two-thirds of the world's population faces a shortage of water for at least one month a year. These shortages affect all continents and all groups of countries, rich and poor alike, but their consequences are more threatening in poor countries.[12]

At this juncture we must distinguish between shortages of fresh water and lack of access to potable water. The two phenomena do not always coincide, even if they often occur in combination. Unsurprisingly, the map of international inequalities of access to potable water resembles the map of income inequalities between countries. More than half of the people without access to potable water in the world live in sub-Saharan Africa. Within these countries income inequality is also very great, with consequences that are plainly incompatible with any conception of social justice. The poorest city dwellers generally can obtain only potable water that is delivered in tanks, at a price five to ten times higher (indeed sometimes as much as twenty times higher in cities such as Dar es Salaam in Tanzania) than that of the water that comes out of the faucets and the hoses watering the gardens of wealthy homes on the edge of the shanty towns.[13] The only substitutes for water from tanks are water from unsafe sources (which causes gastrointestinal infections) or else water from wells (which is not always safe either) that is carried over great distances by women and girls who are left with little time to go to school or to acquire job skills. Inegalitarian access to potable water is thus driven by economic inequalities, as much as it perpetuates and accentuates them, creating a poverty trap for those who fall victim to them.

Unequal Access to Nourishing Foods

As in the case of water and energy, both vital daily needs, access to nourishing foods is restricted by substantial social inequalities. At the very bottom of the scale, persons living in extreme poverty do not have enough to eat. This is a chilling reality not only in emerging countries, but also in rich countries (even in the United States, some three million people are estimated to live in extreme poverty).

Apart from the very poor, everyone in rich countries has enough to eat; no significant social gradient is observed with regard to the quantity of calories consumed. By contrast, there is a strong correlation between income and access to "quality calories" from foods that promote good health, such as fresh fruits, vegetables, and fish. This helps to explain why, in the United States, almost four out of ten people are obese, and why this rate rises to more than 45 percent for women living on less than $890 per month and falls to 30 percent for women living on more than $2,400 per month. In Europe, obesity is less pronounced than in the United States (though it is sharply on the rise), but there too it is to a large degree correlated with income. The percentage of obese adults is almost four times higher in France among households having an income below €900 a month than among those earning more than €5,300 a month.[14]

The underlying reason for this state of affairs is that the price of food increases as nutritional quality for a given caloric content improves: a calorie of organic green beans purchased from a greengrocer is five times more expensive (often much more, in fact) than a calorie of frozen chicken nuggets, for example—increasing the risk of pathologies associated with diets that are often constrained by individual or household budgets. Foods with quality calories are not only more expensive but also less convenient for low-income persons to shop for, since organic food stores are typically located in wealthy neighborhoods. Research has also confirmed that there is a vicious circle linking social inequalities and unequal access to nutritious foods. If the level of income helps to explain the incidence of obesity, obesity also has an effect on income, demonstrated in several countries, in large part because the obese are victims of discrimination in hiring.

Better information, particularly through more specific labelling of food products, is certainly needed if a change in dietary habits is to be brought about, but it is clear too that this cannot be enough. The democratization of wholesome foods depends on lowering the relative cost of these foods and on making access to them more equal, as much as it depends on raising incomes at the bottom of the social scale.

Unequal Access to Territorial Resources

The magisterial work of the economic historian Karl Polyani that I mentioned earlier, *The Great Transformation,* contains a fascinating account of the enclosure movement that grew up during the Tudor period in England.[15] Up to that time, during the Middle Ages, open fields for communal use were an economic resource for small tenant farmers and landless peasants. Beginning in the late sixteenth century, these commons came under private ownership and were enclosed by hedges. The seizure of natural resources, first by lords and nobles, then increasingly by wealthy country gentlemen and merchants, forced the poor to leave their villages and migrate to nearby cities, where living conditions were often even still more uncertain than in the countryside. For Polyani, this movement marked the beginning of the commodification both of labor and of nature, which now became commercial goods like any other, and, by creating the conditions that made the Industrial Revolution possible, portended the birth of modern capitalism.

The social repercussions of commodifying nature were observed in several countries during the Industrial Revolution. Privatization of wooded land with a view to its commercial exploitation, in the forests of Rhenish Prussia in 1821, was a formative influence on the young Karl Marx's thinking about private property. For centuries peasants had been accustomed to collect dead wood and burn it as logs and kindling to heat their homes. But once a market for firewood from which the owners of the land could profit came into existence, this practice was declared illegal on the ground that the wood had been stolen. Marx strenuously objected, arguing in a series of articles published in 1842 that the common law had been both irrationally and unjustly overturned to the advantage of forest owners, which is to say the wealthy classes.[16] Marx went on to develop this theme in the rest of his work.

In France, under the Ancien Régime and after the Revolution, similar conflicts over access to communal goods set property owners and poor farmers against one another. At the dawn of the Industrial Revolution, there were still undivided lands the nobility had not yet succeeded in appropriating on which landless peasants were free to graze their animals. But in the period of rapid economic transformation that followed, this arrangement was decidedly not to the liking of the central government. In the mid-nineteenth century, it took the view that common pasture lands in Grenoble, in the French Alps, were an unproductive use of resources and sought to force communes to sell them. The municipal council, alert to the inegalitarian implications of such sales, defended the common lands on the ground that they benefitted the poorest (the "unhappiest," as they were called at the time). Under pressure from the state, however, the council ended up agreeing to the sale of the lands. Such privatizations occurred in many other locations.

Unfortunately, the tragedy of the commons illustrated by these historical examples is being reenacted in many parts of the world today. Much the same thing is happening with mangrove forests, the rich ecosystems that grow up around coastal marshes. In Central and South America and Southeast Asia, the privatization of public lands has allowed mangroves to be transformed into shrimp farming zones, typically with the justification that the new industry creates jobs and stimulates regional economic development. But many studies, particularly those conducted by the Spanish economist Joan Martínez Alier on the impact of privatization policies in Ecuador, Sri Lanka, Indonesia, and Malaysia, have shown that entire communities whose subsistence had always depended on these natural resources have been evicted from coastal areas to make way for the construction of shrimp-processing facilities.[17] They have therefore not only been deprived of their livelihood, but dispossessed of their social and cultural heritage as well.

In the meantime, the economic gains from shrimp farming have been largely concentrated in the hands of the farm owners. Their businesses thrive at the expense of the environment, which is damaged by pollution from the antibiotics used in managing shrimp ponds and by the destruction of local fishing grounds. Under pressure from ecologists in countries importing farm-raised shrimp, certification labels have been awarded to producers who respect accepted standards of responsible aquaculture, but this has not prevented ruinous management practices from continuing in some places.

This type of conflict also poses questions concerning the standard of measurement used to evaluate the services rendered by ecosystems (in the way of diet, health, protection against coastal erosion, and so on) and the relative benefits of any alternatives that may be proposed. Do gains from commerce in shrimp compensate for the losses caused by the destruction of mangroves? To measure these losses, is it necessary to monetize the services rendered by mangroves or to use other types of indicators?

The choice of a method for evaluating different options is decisive in such cases. The same problem arises in connection with many environmental conflicts throughout the world: in India, with the construction of nuclear power plants, notably the Kudankulam station in Tamil Nadu; in France, with the controversial plan (eventually abandoned) to build a large airport in the commune of Nôtre-Dame-des-Landes, outside Nantes; in North America, with the ongoing battle over the Keystone XL pipeline. On the one hand, benefits are reckoned in terms of jobs and economic growth; on the other, costs are reckoned in terms of potential damage to public health, biodiversity, the climate, and, more generally, the well-being of the planet.

I shall come back to this point in Part Three. For the moment let us note that the measurement of costs and benefits associated with an environmental service, far from being neutral, is a political act through and through. Whoever manages to impose or to win acceptance for a certain system of measurement is very likely to prevail in public debate.

4

Unequal Exposure to Environmental Risks

INEQUALITIES in regard to environmental risks (such as drought) or environmental degradation (such as air pollution) are the reverse of inequalities involving environmental resources. Inequalities of access and exposure may, of course, go hand in hand: in the case of the mangroves we considered in Chapter 3, resource privatization is accompanied by soil contamination. But it is useful to distinguish between these two forms of inequality because their mechanisms are different.

Disparities in exposure to environmental risks have a dual character. Socially disadvantaged groups are, in general, more likely to be directly affected (they live closer to the sites of industrial pollution, frequently in flood zones as well), and they are also more vulnerable to injury from such risks.[1] In the case of environmental catastrophes, the economically less well-off have fewer material means to cope with their effects. In the case of various kinds of pollution that cause health problems, it is generally harder for the poor to have screening tests done and to receive medical treatment.[2] As we will see, these two factors interact and, in combination, serve to reinforce socioeconomic inequalities.

Socioenvironmental Health Inequalities

The observed increase in the risk of contracting chronic illnesses such as cardiovascular disease, diabetes, and cancer results mainly from modifications of living conditions and the environment. The term *exposome* is used to characterize the set of nongenetic risk factors, including liability to contamination from external sources, internal biological dispositions (e.g., gut microflora) and lifestyle (diet, physical exercise, stress, and so on), that may induce pathologies. The American researchers Stephen Rappaport and Martyn Smith estimate that these factors account for between 70 and 90 percent of the risk of contracting a chronic illness.[3]

LEAD POISONING

In the United States, environmental inequalities are sometimes identified with racial injustice in view of the fact, long documented by government agencies, academic researchers, and private advocacy groups, that black Americans live closer to hazardous waste landfills and industrial centers than whites do.[4] A team led by the American economist Anna Aizer found that these inequalities of exposure to environmental degradation principally harm the health of the most disadvantaged, and this from early childhood, thus perpetuating a vicious circle of poverty and inequality throughout a person's life.[5]

The study conducted by Aizer and her colleagues concerns lead poisoning, also known by its ancient name, saturnism (derived from the alchemic name for lead). Saturnism is a disease that has all but disappeared in several European countries, but that still exists over the globe, particularly on the other side of the Atlantic.[6] In children, ingestion of even small amounts of lead may be enough to poison the organism and disturb the nervous system, impairing cognitive abilities and therefore limiting the chance of normal development later in life. The researchers sought to measure the effect of lead exposure on disparities in educational performance. Their sample consisted of more than sixty thousand children in the state of Rhode Island over a period of more than ten years, from 1997 to 2010. Although Rhode Island is relatively egalitarian by comparison with the national standard, African Americans in that state recorded lower test scores than those of whites (eight on a scale of twenty, on average, as opposed to ten) and they were clearly more exposed to lead than whites (roughly 60 percent more in 1997), because they lived in disproportionate numbers in dilapidated housing.

Analysis of the data clearly shows that black children are more liable than white children to develop saturnism and less likely to do well in school. This does not allow us to assert with confidence that saturnism is responsible for the observed differences in educational achievement, however. Other independent factors may link the two inequalities. The level of education of a child's parents, for example, may explain worse scholastic performance and at the same time be associated with exposure to lead: poorly educated parents have, on average, lower incomes, and therefore are likelier to live in apartments with high lead levels; additionally, they have fewer resources to help their children succeed in school. This might account for much of the correlation between lead and poor grades, without lead itself being responsible for scholastic inequalities.

Let us now examine how Aizer and her team managed to demonstrate that there is in fact a causal link between the two forms of inequality. In order to test their hypothesis, evidently it was not possible to make a randomly selected group of children ingest a certain quantity of lead and to compare, year by year, their test results with those of a control group that had not been poisoned. What to do then? The researchers used a technique that is extremely useful in the medical and social sciences known as instrumental variables estimation. It was necessary first to find a suitable variable (an "instrument") that can be shown to have causal effect only on lead exposure, not on test results. Next, it was necessary to observe in what proportions test results were influenced by the changes in this variable.

The instrumental variable they chose was a government regulation prohibiting the use of certain kinds of lead-based paint in apartments. Unavoidably this regulation had a very clear effect on lead exposure, but by itself it had none on test scores, since laws concerning lead content in no way directly affect the desire or ability to learn. The only effect it could have on test scores would therefore be through lower rates of saturnism, that is, through a reduction in rates of exposure to lead. If the regulation's effect on lead exposure could be measured, together with changes in test scores once the new rule had come into force, it would then be possible to measure the effect of lead exposure on test scores. Disparities in scholastic performance would therefore be solely due to lead exposure, without interference from any other variable (see Figure 4.1).

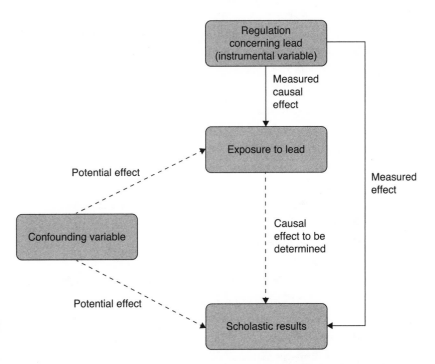

Figure 4.1. Measuring inequalities in lead exposure. Variation in school performance due to the regulation concerning lead can be measured, as well as the regulation's effect on lead exposure (solid lines); by contrast, the effect of lead exposure on school performance (dotted lines) cannot be directly measured. *Sources and series:* www.lucaschancel.info/hup.

In Rhode Island, the regulation had a nontrivial effect in reducing the black-white gap in lead exposure: in the seven years following its enactment, overexposure of African American households fell from 60 percent in 1997 to 38 percent in 2004. What is more, the narrowing of this gap was accompanied by a clear improvement in African American test scores. Using the method just described, the researchers were able to demonstrate that about a half of the reduction in unequal scholastic performance over the entire period, 1997–2010, was due to the reduction in environmental inequality brought about by the new regulation. It needs to be kept in mind that African Americans are still subject to higher levels of lead exposure than whites (as illustrated by the more recent case of Newark's water crisis). If this difference were entirely eliminated, it is very probable that the gap in test scores would be further reduced.

Unfortunately, health problems associated with many other forms of unequal exposure to environmental risks in the United States have yet to be addressed—and the list grows longer every year. Polybrominated diphenyl ether (PBDE), for example, is a chemical used in the manufacture of a wide array of products, including plastics and textiles, that affects the nervous system in children and disrupts brain development. The level of exposure to PBDE among African Americans is twice that among whites—again, very probably owing to the greater proximity of homes to factories.[7]

A crucial issue for public policy is to identify the areas and the populations exposed to pollutants as well as to different types of pollution. As we will see in Part Three, publicly accessible cartographic tools have been devised in recent years to inform environmental regulation and to assist the enforcement of new rules. Before the election of Donald Trump and his dim-witted assault on environmental policy, the United States led the way in disseminating information about pollution. European countries, although they often claim to be at the forefront of efforts to protect the environment, have still a long way to go in making the new cartographic tools available to their citizens. In the emerging world this crucial issue seems to be off the radar of civil society and political parties' platforms.

Atmospheric pollution is responsible for more than four million deaths per year, according to the World Health Organization (WHO), through an increased risk of heart attack as well as lung cancer and other chronic respiratory diseases due to penetration of the organism by the fine particulate matter emitted by fuel combustion and waste incineration.[8]

Some idea of the size of these microscopic particles may be had by imagining a magnitude one-tenth the thickness of a human hair in diameter. The shorthand for such particles, having a diameter of ten microns or less, is PM_{10}.[9] The most dangerous ones are those in the $PM_{2.5}$ class, having a size of 2.5 microns or less, equivalent to a fortieth of the width of our hypothetical hair. The smaller the particle, the more damagingly it can penetrate tissues and organs because it can go deep inside them.

Emerging countries with large low-income populations are the most vulnerable to ambient air pollution. According to the WHO, the annual average concentration of $PM_{2.5}$ should be lower than ten micrograms per cubic meter of air and should not exceed twenty-five micrograms more than three days per year. New Delhi, until very recently the most polluted city in the world, has annual averages fluctuating around 100 micrograms per cubic meter, with daily peaks exceeding the highest three-figure measurement that sensors are capable of registering, 999 micrograms per cubic meter (the equivalent of smoking fifty cigarettes a day).

While air pollution in the metropolitan areas of emerging countries frequently reaches astronomical levels, the risks associated with this kind of pollution are far from negligible in rich countries. In France, for example, pollution in the form of fine particulate matter emitted by diesel combustion and other carbon-based fuels is responsible for 9 percent of all deaths, a considerable number. It represents fifty thousand deaths per year—equivalent to the number of deaths caused by alcohol abuse in this country. In terms of life expectancy at the age of thirty, a French person would gain an average of nine months if there were no fine-particle pollution.[10]

Moments when regulatory warning thresholds are exceeded—so-called pollution peaks—make the front page of newspapers and provoke an outpouring of concern from politicians once or twice a year in various European countries. But they are not the biggest killers; a far greater danger is regular exposure throughout the year, which even in relatively small doses is lethal. In the case of France, about thirty-five thousand of its fifty thousand fatalities could be avoided if the towns that are most affected were to bring their pollution levels down to those of the towns that are the least affected. To put it another way, seven deaths out of every hundred in France each year could be prevented if all French towns had the same low incidence of pollution.

All social classes are affected by air pollution, but the poor are generally the first victims. One of the reasons for this is that the areas where pollution is highest are typically where low-income persons live. In the United States, coal-fired power plants that spew fine particles into the air in massive quantities are overrepresented in the vicinity of neighborhoods inhabited by African Americans: 76 percent of those who live next to the twelve most polluting plants are nonwhite. If exposure to the risks associated with such plants were equally distributed with regard to race, this figure would only be 28 percent.[11] The term *environmental racism,* often used by civil rights groups and environmental justice organizations in the United States, has its origin in such findings.

Moreover, even in areas where unequal exposure to pollution is not observed, the poorest individuals are generally at greatest risk. A team of French researchers led by Séverine Deguen has studied the differential effects of fine-particle pollution in Paris.[12] Although poor neighborhoods are not disproportionally exposed to atmospheric pollution (contrary to what the city's history would lead one to expect, since fashionable neighborhoods sprang up in areas sheltered from the noxious fumes emitted by factories), the homes of the wealthiest are generally less polluted (they have better ventilation systems and now, in many cases, air conditioning). Poor residents also spend more time in subways and buses, where pollution is greater than in their homes.

A second reason is that an individual's level of health is correlated with income (recall the ten "solid facts" mentioned in Chapter 1). As a consequence, the poorest are the most vulnerable to the effects of urban pollution.

Third, and finally, the wealthiest Parisians have other means to protect themselves against pollution, by making weekend visits to their country houses in Normandy or Champagne-Ardenne, for example, which reduces their rate of exposure over the course of the year. All the evidence suggests that very strong corroboration of these results could be obtained in cities such as New Delhi and Lagos, where the difference in levels of household air pollution between the rich and less rich is still more glaring.

HOUSEHOLD AIR POLLUTION

Even within the same households, not everyone is equal in the face of air pollution. This is especially the case in developing countries, where indoor air pollution is particularly high owing to customary methods of heating water and cooking. In 2017, in the developing world as a whole, three billion people used traditional sources of energy for cooking. Burning wood or wood charcoal for these purposes generates the very microparticles that are responsible for the outdoor pollution discussed above.

Here gender inequality is combined with socioeconomic inequality: fine-particle household pollution primarily affects women and children, who spend more time indoors at home than men. Women and children are thus more likely to suffer from lung disease (half of the deaths due to pediatric pneumonia are caused by the poor quality of household air), and cardiac disorders, which together account for four million deaths per year worldwide (or about 7 percent of deaths from all causes), almost exclusively in developing and emerging countries.[13]

AGRICULTURAL AND INDUSTRIAL POLLUTION

Air pollution attracts wide media attention, in part because it is actually visible during peak periods. But contamination of soil and water, which adversely affects the health of everyone, particularly the poorest, must not be forgotten. Pesticides and herbicides are an important factor in the inegalitarian effects of agricultural and industrial pollution. Their principal victims are farmers and workers who regularly come into contact with these substances through the skin (from handling them directly), the mouth (from smoking after having handled them), and the respiratory system (from inhaling the fumes produced by spraying), as well as their families and closest neighbors. Exposure to pesticides strongly increases the risk of contracting cancers of the prostate and skin as well as neurodegenerative illnesses such as Parkinson's disease.[14] While the effects of toxic substances on health are now better understood, thanks to advances in medical research, and more effectively counteracted, thanks to new legislation and court rulings, further progress has been hindered by manufacturers that are able to invest massively in large-scale disinformation campaigns. The agrochemical giant Monsanto, however, has already been obliged to pay substantial fines in both France and the United States for deceptive advertising; in addition, thousands of lawsuits—many of which are still pending—have been brought against the company for past and present malfeasance. The firm has been ordered to pay more than two billion dollars to victims so far, although certain cases will be subject to appellate review.

Finally, it has been established that those who are most exposed to risk from pollution associated with pesticides and herbicides are also more vulnerable than the average person. Several studies show that farmers in many countries have less access to screening tests and medical care than the national average.[15]

So far we have mostly limited our attention to inequalities among individuals, but the spatial dimension is nonetheless a crucial element of the link between income level and risk exposure. Whole territories can be contaminated by human activities. One thinks in this connection of mining areas (the basins of northern Europe, for example, and the American states of Alaska, Utah, and Nevada) where many cases of soil and water contamination by heavy metals are documented. Notwithstanding the lack of systematic studies of soil screening levels in most developing countries, extractive industries there are known to produce at least as much damage as in the mining areas of rich countries, since legal regulations are typically less stringent and extractive industries' practices are often more ruinous.[16]

Unequal Exposure to Environmental Shocks

Chronic illnesses brought about by various forms of pollution I have just discussed generally develop over a long period. In the case of environmental shocks caused by hurricanes, tornados, droughts, or floods, by contrast, exposure is immediate. Their effects, as we will see, are for the most part unequally distributed as well—even if, let us not forget, everyone is hurt by them, rich and poor alike. Let us recall, too, that the term often used to designate these events, *natural catastrophes,* is misleading: almost three-quarters of the drought events observed in the world today are associated with climate change, itself due to human activity.[17] Natural catastrophes are therefore not as natural as the language suggests.

In 2005, Hurricane Katrina struck Louisiana and its major city, New Orleans. It proved to be one of the most costly environmental catastrophes in the history of the United States, with damages estimated at more than $100 billion. Katrina was responsible for almost two thousand deaths and remains still today a powerful reminder of the social, environmental, and ethnic divisions that beset the world's greatest economic power. The television series *Treme*, set in a mostly black working-class neighborhood of New Orleans after the storm, vividly illustrates not only the hardships endured by the city's inhabitants, but also the unequal access to funds for recovery and rebuilding.[18]

The failure of the levees during the storm made the difference in exposure to risk between blacks and whites plain for all to see: half of the city's black population lived in stricken areas; only thirty percent of the white population did. To put the matter another way, the risk for blacks was 68 percent greater than for whites. This is explained in part by the fact that the city's flood zones coincide mainly with poor neighborhoods having a high proportion of African American residents. The highest land, occupied on the whole by whites, many of them well-off, was much better protected against flooding.

In addition to this inequality of exposure there were differences in vulnerability to the damage caused by the storm. I need not repeat here that the health of the poorest is worse than the average. In New Orleans, another factor came into play: resilience, which is to say the ability to withstand shocks. Many African American families were unable to get out before the storm hit because they did not have a car. More than half of the people interviewed by the researcher François Gemenne who did not leave the city told him that they stayed because they had no means of transportation.[19] This situation is encountered in many countries. In England, the less well-off are more exposed to the risk of injury from coastal flooding: among the poorest 10 percent, about one in six lives in a flood zone, as opposed to only one in a hundred among the wealthiest 10 percent.[20] The same is true on a global scale. More than 2.5 billion people live within one hundred kilometers of a coastline; more than three-quarters of them live in a developing country.

This state of affairs is not limited to flood risk. The French economist Stéphane Hallegatte and his colleagues at the World Bank have shown that the poorest are more exposed to environmental shocks in a majority of cases studied in Africa, Asia, and Latin America.[21] Furthermore, the less well-off are always more vulnerable to injury from these shocks. The authors advance two reasons for this. First, housing, transportation, and other goods within the means of the poorest are less resistant to shocks than are the resources enjoyed by the wealthiest. Second, when a catastrophe occurs (whether environmental or not), it is liable to destroy whatever resources the poorest have. The wealthiest, by contrast, do not store all their assets in the same place; some are deposited in banks, for example.

To sum up, we have seen that in many countries the poor are overrepresented in areas at greatest risk, whether from air pollution, soil contamination, flood, or drought. And yet there is no absolute correspondence between income levels and exposure to environmental risk. The territorial dimension of these issues is apt to obscure the effect of social inequalities: when an area is affected by pollution or struck by a devastating storm, people from all walks of life are victims in one way or another. This acts as a basic reminder that we are all concerned by environmental damage.

Nevertheless there can be no question that the poor are more vulnerable to such shocks, because they lack the means to protect themselves against them. Once again we encounter a vicious circle in which economic, environmental, and political inequalities are mutually reinforcing. Modern societies are characterized by an inegalitarian distribution of environmental risk and of the resources necessary to withstand its worst effects. In its turn, this state of affairs inevitably strengthens preexisting social inequalities.

5

Unequal Responsibility
for Pollution

HAVING EXAMINED inequalities of access to resources and of exposure to risks, we must now consider a third facet of environmental inequality: the responsibility of polluters for the damages they cause. At once a problem arises. Are we to think about this inequality in the context of disparities between countries, or between industrial sectors, or between individuals? Who is responsible, for example, for the pollution produced in making this book? The author? The publisher? The printer and binder? The company that ships copies to the warehouse? The reader? These questions raise a number of ethical problems in their turn. We will have to say precisely what kind of responsibility we are talking about before we can analyze inequalities of responsibility, and then, in Part Three, consider what responses can be given.

The Problem of Environmental Responsibility

The term *Anthropocene* was coined to describe the geological era we are living in today, one in which human activity modifies the geoclimatic system, by contrast with previous eras during which only geophysical forces were capable of altering the climate.[1] While there is still some controversy among geophysicists regarding the term's usefulness, it is undeniable that the climate system, under the influence of human action upon it, is being disrupted with stunning rapidity, the like of which was unknown until the present age. The notion of an Anthropocene era therefore has the virtue of directly confronting human beings with their responsibility for the derangement of planetary stability and for its long-term consequences. But we must not forget that human beings do not constitute a compact, homogeneous group whose members all contribute to this unprecedented upheaval in the same manner and to the same degree.

Another way of thinking about the current ecological crisis is to look at it as a matter of transgenerational justice. On this view, climate disruption is an injustice that unfolds over time and, by virtue of just this, sets succeeding generations against one another. This perspective forms the basis of the influential Stern Review, released by the government of the United Kingdom in 2006, which reckoned the cost of climate change for our generation and those that come after us to be about 15 percent of global gross domestic product (GDP) and the cost of preventing its most catastrophic effects to be somewhere between 1 and 2 percent.[2] Stern's calculations, however approximate they may have been, were valuable for giving politicians, journalists, and scholars a clearer idea of the future impact of climate change and the immense injustice that will be inflicted on those who come after us if nothing is done. But there is much more to climate change than this. Within any given generation, there are winners and losers—polluters and victims of pollution, which is to say those who dominate politically and those who are dominated.

A third way of looking at the matter, the prevailing view in international climate negotiations up until now, contrasts countries—or groups of countries—with one another. Comparing the map of countries having the highest levels of carbon dioxide emissions with the map of countries that are most vulnerable to the consequences of climate change makes it plain that the greatest polluters (measured by average per capita emissions) are also the least exposed to the effects of climate change. Again, however, we are faced with a number of questions.

Do historical levels of emissions and current data need to be taken into consideration in order to attribute degrees of responsibility? Should we be looking at per capita levels or a country's total emissions? At emissions associated with household consumption or all emissions produced over a country's entire territory? And should we not also take into consideration a country's income and its capacity to act (on the ground that countries that *can* act have a greater duty to act than those that cannot)? Figure 5.1 compares current and historical levels of emissions with national shares of gross world product on a global scale. The European Union, for example, accounts for 11 percent of current emissions, but 16 percent of global GDP and almost 20 percent of historical emissions. This profile is reversed in the case of China, which

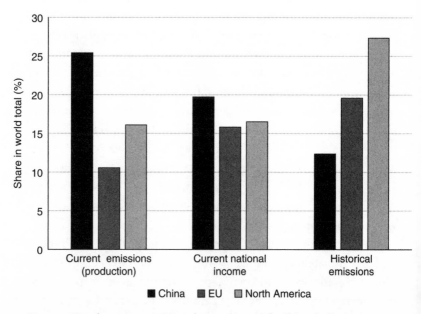

Figure 5.1. Greenhouse gas emissions and national income for China, the European Union, and North America. China is responsible for 25 percent of current world greenhouse gas emissions (associated with industrial production) and 12 percent of historic emissions, and accounts for 20 percent of world national income. *Sources and series:* www.lucaschancel.info/hup.

accounts for more than 25 percent of current emissions and less than 13 percent of historical emissions. What principle must be adopted if we are to fairly evaluate contributions and responsibilities in each case?

At the Kyoto Climate Change Conference, in 1997, negotiators reached agreement on a principle of "common but differentiated responsibilities" (CBDR). This amounted to officially accepting that all countries are responsible for climate change, but that only those that historically have significantly contributed to it and that have high standards of living ("Annex I Parties") are obligated to reduce their greenhouse gas emissions. The Kyoto Protocol therefore distinguishes two categories: the Annex I Parties (consisting at the time of Organisation for Economic Co-operation and Development member countries, together with so-called economies in transition), and the rest of the world. The Protocol therefore combines two notions of justice: responsibility based on historical and current emissions (corrective justice) and responsibility based on national income and the capacity to pay (distributive justice).

This dual approach to the question of responsibility is still being pursued today in international climate negotiations. The understanding of global climate justice formalized by the Kyoto Protocol lives on, for example, in the finance provisions of the 2015 Paris Agreement: only industrial countries are obligated to contribute to the fund of $100 billion to be reserved for adapting to climate change; others can contribute if they wish to do so.

The negotiators did not wish to explicitly call into question the principles agreed upon at Kyoto, for fear of derailing the entire process at a moment of mounting tensions among the parties. The Paris talks had reached an impasse in trying to come to terms with one of the outstanding facts of the world today: inequalities in standards of living are both considerable and increasing within countries. In that case, ought not wealthy South Africans, Chinese, Brazilians, Russians, and Indians likewise be called upon to help mitigate global warming in proportion to their contribution to current levels of pollution? In the scheme ratified at Kyoto, however, only national averages count, not variations among income groups within countries.

A few weeks prior to the 2015 United Nations Climate Change Conference (COP 21), which took place in Paris in late 2015, Thomas Piketty and I published a study that invited negotiators and the general public to put individual responsibility back at the heart of debate.[3] It seemed to us that by exposing the fantasy of sustainable development a way could be found to put an end to the stalemate.

The Myth of an Environmental Kuznets Curve

Earlier I mentioned the naïve claim that has sometimes been made on the basis of the Kuznets curve, namely, that income inequalities will mechanically be reduced as a country develops. A similar relation between pollution and the level of development was asserted by the economists Gene Grossman and Alan Krueger more than twenty-five years ago.[4] They argued that when a country is in the early stages of development, growth through urbanization and the construction of roads and factories occurs at the expense of ecosystems and air quality—the collateral damage of industrialization, as it were. The population will accept this trade-off to begin with, regarding it as a regrettable but unavoidable cost of modernization, but as the standard of living improves more time and resources will be dedicated to protecting the environment. Eventually a tipping point will be reached when, on a global scale, collective investment in ecologically sustainable technologies is seen to be both desirable and feasible. This is the so-called environmental Kuznets curve, which is also asserted to obtain at the individual level: beyond a certain level of income, people are more willing to eat organic foods, buy electric cars, insulate their homes, and so on, with the result that pollution levels will decline even among the wealthiest.

Grossman and Krueger's conjecture holds great appeal for governments primarily concerned with promoting economic development.

No need to worry about the environment—so long as the right growth policies are put in place, it will take care of itself. Alas, this is a myth. The famous bell curve has been confirmed in various countries only for a few pollutants. With regard to a majority of the most harmful pollutants, particularly greenhouse gases, and with regard to water and land-use requirements for satisfying rising levels of household consumption demand, no such pattern has been observed.[5]

Will Wealth Destroy the Planet?

Comparing individuals rather than countries, we observe growing use of most pollutants as income increases. Here I shall focus on CO_2 and the greenhouse gases classified as carbon dioxide equivalents (CO_2e), not because the harms caused by other forms of pollution are insignificant, but because greenhouse gases represent one of the greatest challenges presently facing humanity. Moreover, we now have fairly detailed information concerning these gases, which makes it easier to study inequalities of responsibility.

Studies involving many countries have shown that income (or level of expenditure, which is closely associated with income) is the principal factor explaining differences in CO_2 emissions among individuals in a given country.[6] Here, as in connection with energy consumption, it is necessary to distinguish between direct and indirect emissions. Direct emissions are produced at the site where energy is used (by a gas furnace, for example, or a car's exhaust system). Indirect emissions are a consequence of producing goods and services that are consumed—smartphones, organic carrots, movies. The things that we use every day, in other words, could not have been invented, manufactured, transported, or sold without energy. This kind of emission may be produced domestically or, in the case of imports, abroad. We will see in what follows that taking imported indirect emissions into account substantially modifies the classical distribution of CO_2 emissions among countries.

We saw in Chapter 3 that individuals' energy consumption increases with income, but less than proportionally. This is also the case with CO_2 emissions, which result from energy usage. Direct emissions tend to increase as incomes rise, but less than proportionally. There is a limit to the amount of heat we need each day and to the volume of gasoline that we can put in our car (those who have several cars cannot drive them all at once). By contrast, there is no such limit to the amount of goods and services that money can buy. Cars sitting in a garage all day do not add to direct CO_2 emissions, but the cost of their manufacture must be taken into account and amortized on their owner's balance sheet day after day. Indirect emissions are therefore more closely tied to income than are direct emissions. The wealthier the individual, the greater his share of indirect emissions: for the richest 20 percent in France and America, they make up three-quarters of their total emissions, as against two-thirds for the poorest 20 percent.[7]

The available evidence shows that total emissions, or the sum of direct and indirect emissions, do not decrease with income within countries: they clearly increase, although generally a little less rapidly than income. More precisely, when income increases by 1 percent, carbon emissions increase within a range of 0.6 percent to very slightly more than 1 percent, depending on the country, with a median value of about 0.9 percent. The figure linking increases in income with increases in emissions is called "income-emissions elasticity."

Very sizable levels of emissions inequality are nonetheless observed. In the United States, for example, average CO_2e emissions are twenty-three metric tons annually per person; but the poorest 50 percent emit about thirteen metric tons of CO_2e per year and the wealthiest 1 percent emit at least 150 metric tons.[8] This disparity is the result of a very energy-intensive model of consumption (even at the bottom of the social ladder) with high levels of income and consumption dispersion. This stands in contrast to the French case, where the appetite for carbon of society as a whole is much more moderate (largely thanks to more efficient transportation and heating and cooling energy systems) and where much lower average emissions are recorded for the poorer half: on the order of six metric tons of CO_2e compared to about eighty metric tons for the top 1 percent. In Brazil, the bottom 50 percent emit about 1.6 metric tons of CO_2e per capita, compared to seventy or so metric tons for the top 1 percent. Here, and in other emerging countries, whereas a large part of the population is responsible for low to very low levels of pollution, the energy consumption of an economic elite, at least among the top 1 percent, approaches that of rich Europeans and North Americans.

Beyond Income

Income explains the greater part of the variation in emissions observed among individuals, but many other variables come into play—for example, personal preferences regarding diet and vacation destinations. But it is not always a question of individual choices; some people have high emission levels because of so-called technical constraints (their homes are energy gluttons), or political constraints (public transportation where they live is inadequate). We may distinguish three types of factors, in addition to income, that influence emissions: technical, spatial, and sociocultural.

Among technical factors, the choice of electrical and energy equipment (home heating systems, thermal insulation, household appliances, cars, and so on) has a considerable impact on greenhouse gas emissions. Thus, for example, assuming an equal standard of living, between a household equipped with the most energy-efficient appliances and another enjoying the same level of service but using twenty-year-old equipment, direct CO_2e emissions vary by a factor of three (and total emissions by about 20 percent).[9]

The geography and economic organization of metropolitan areas also have an effect. It takes four times more direct energy per inhabitant to get around an American city than a European city, owing to stricter city planning codes and more severe spatial constraints in Europe. Note that this state of affairs is not only a consequence of individual decisions (whether or not to replace a furnace, for example), but also of collective political choices (or failures to choose). No one can construct a new railway line by himself, or integrate residential neighborhoods with downtown business districts. Geography and climate also help to explain differences in heating and ventilation: a lowering of outdoor temperature by one degree leads to a 5 percent increase in direct energy consumption in France.[10]

Finally, sociocultural factors, such as household size (the more members, the less carbon is emitted per capita since economies of scale can be realized when resource use is shared) and educational levels, need to be taken into consideration in reckoning an individual's total consumption. In France, the level of education explains a large share of the differences in transport-related emissions, as those who are more educated tend to travel more at a given income level.[11] This can affect total emissions. A French commuter emits on average 0.7 metric tons of CO_2e per year in driving from home to work and back; a single Paris–New York flight emits twice this amount.

The Baby-Boomer Effect

In a study of direct greenhouse gas emissions in the United States and France, I looked at the generational effect on carbon emissions.[12] Do younger generations emit more than their elders, and what factors explain differences between generations throughout their lives? To answer these questions it is necessary to sift through data concerning individual energy consumption over several decades, which can now be done more efficiently than before thanks to the growing number of studies on household consumption and to the existence of digital databases on energy use.

Let us first consider the case of the United States. Here no substantial generational effect is observed: all age cohorts emit large amounts of carbon throughout their lifetime; birth dates do not influence the level of total emissions. Indeed, young people emit as much as older people do. This may seem paradoxical since, in value surveys, younger Americans declare they care more about the environment than their parents. We would do well to keep in mind that words are apt to be disconnected from actions when it comes to ecological behavior.

In France, by contrast, the generational effect on carbon is clear. Over the course of their lives, baby boomers and members of the preceding generation (born between 1935 and 1950) tend to emit more direct carbon emissions than both their parents and their children—between 15 and 20 percent more than the average (Figure 5.2).

This is an interesting result, for it is a consequence of the various forces acting on carbon emissions that we just looked at. About a quarter of the generational gap is due to the relatively high incomes

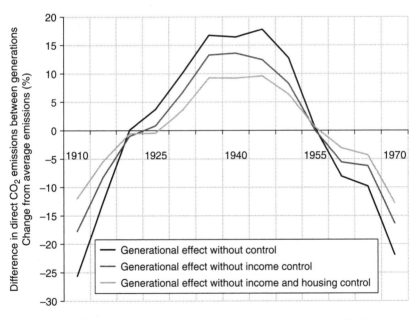

Figure 5.2. Pollution inequalities and generational effects in France, 1910–1980. The figure shows the gap in CO2 emissions between a generation born at a given date and the average generation born between 1910 and 1980. Baby boomers born in 1940 emit 10 percent to 17 percent more than the average. *Sources and series:* www.lucaschancel.info/hup.

enjoyed by baby boomers throughout their lives. This is still more true in France than in the United States: baby boomers found jobs from a very early age in France, at a time when income growth was robust. When we compare them at the same age, we find that French men and women born in 1945 were relatively better off than their children. The income gap between those aged 30–35 years and those aged 50–55 years was 15 percent in 1977, as opposed to 40 percent in 2009. From these differences in income flow differences in CO_2e emissions: baby boomers use more heat in their homes, consume more gasoline, and travel more than other generations at the same age.[13]

But income alone is not enough to explain the baby-boomer effect. The difference between this generation and the others is explained also by the energy characteristics of the houses and apartments they occupy. Baby boomers entered the real-estate market at a time when heating and insulation systems were relatively inefficient; what is more, these systems remained in service for a good many years, in some cases even until the present day. This generation was therefore stuck with the infrastructure it had inherited; renovation was a long process stretching out over several generations.

Taken together, income and residential energy efficiency explain half of the difference between baby boomers and adjacent generations. The remaining half is trickier to analyze statistically. It may be due to social norms and a mental outlook peculiar to the generation born after the war; at all events, baby boomers exhibit less virtuous behaviors than their parents, who had endured wartime rationing, among other hardships, and their children, who were born after the oil shocks of the 1970s. In France, as in the United States, younger people today say that they care more about the fate of the environment than their parents do. And yet, as we have seen, the lower emissions levels observed for this generation in France are partly a consequence of economic constraints, not solely of a widespread fear of ecological crisis. This is not altogether reassuring news.

The better news is that the factors that, in addition to income, determine the level of greenhouse gas emissions can be acted on in order to reduce emissions. But we have also seen that these factors are secondary by comparison with differences in income. The whole issue, from the point of view of public policy, is whether a radical transformation can be brought about—of transportation infrastructure, heating and thermal insulation systems, and, above all, the way people think about energy use—in order to sever the link between income levels and greenhouse gas emissions.

Inequalities of Global CO_2e Emissions

Now that we have a clearer sense of the factors that determine levels of individual emissions within countries, it becomes possible to draw a truly global map of ecological obligations by eliminating national boundaries. Where are the high carbon emitters found and where are the low emitters found? How has the geography of pollution inequalities changed in recent years? To what extent has it modified the geopolitics of climate responsibility?

In 2007, American and Indian researchers launched a debate that has caused much ink to be spilled since.[14] The question was whether, at world climate conferences, negotiators from India and emerging countries in general used very low average emission levels for their countries in order to conceal very substantial emissions by the wealthiest class in these countries—which is to say precisely their own class, since these representatives almost invariably come from the upper levels of society.

Two years later the physicist Shoibal Chakravarty and a group of colleagues, physicists and economists at Princeton, published a pioneering study on the subject that measured global inequalities in individual emissions of carbon dioxide.[15] The difficulty they faced in trying to determine the impact of each social group on a global scale was that reliable information on individual emissions was available only for a few countries. The only alternative, then, was to estimate these emissions on the basis of much more comprehensive data on income inequality: on energy intensity; or total energy consumption per unit GDP (some countries have similar income levels but very different emission levels, having made different policy choices with regard to energy); and on income-carbon elasticity (a measurement that allows carbon dioxide emissions to be statistically correlated with income, as we saw earlier). One of the limitations of their study, however, is that it takes into account neither indirect emissions generated abroad nor greenhouse gas emissions as a whole (including methane, nitrous oxide, fluorinated gases, hydrofluorocarbons, and perfluorocarbons in addition to carbon dioxide). Moreover, it does not pay sufficient attention to extreme levels of economic inequality observed

Table 5.1. CO_2e emissions per capita around the world, 2013

	Annual total CO_2e per person (MT)	Difference (in %) in relation to production-based emissions alone	Annual per capita emissions ratio to world average
World average	6.2	0	1.0
North America	22.5	13	3.6
Western Europe	13.1	41	2.1
Middle East	7.4	−8	1.2
China	6.0	−25	1.0
Latin America	4.4	−15	0.7
South Asia	2.2	−8	0.4
Africa	1.9	−21	0.3
Sustainable level	1.2	0	0.2

Note: In 2013, annual total consumption-based emissions per person in North America amounted to 22.5 metric tons total CO_2e, 13 percent more than production-based emissions in North America and 3.6 times the global average. *Sources and series:* www.lucaschancel.info/hup.

within countries, and it tells us nothing about the historical evolution of emissions.

My 2015 study on carbon and inequality, in collaboration with Thomas Piketty, sought to remedy these shortcomings by taking into account indirect and CO_2e emissions as well as economic inequalities. This made it possible to have a more precise idea of the actual distribution of responsibility for climate change. Table 5.1 shows the importance of taking into account emissions produced abroad. The method and the data used also make it possible to trace the evolution of emissions between the Kyoto Protocol of 1997 and the draft framework approved in 2013 for the Paris Agreement.

We used detailed information from the WID.world database on income inequality at the summit of the social pyramid, then combined this with figures for direct and indirect emissions in different parts of the world, while making several assumptions about the link between carbon and income (adjusting elasticity values as necessary), in order to attribute to each social class a share of total emissions. In the end we were able to simulate the emissions of more than 90 percent of the world's population. Improvements can still be made to the methodology—with regard both to adequately accounting for very high incomes and to expanding the measure of carbon dioxide to include all equivalent greenhouse gases—but the results so far obtained are illuminating. Three principal conclusions can be drawn at this point.

First, it is apparent that CO_2e emissions inequality decreased across countries but increased within them between 1998 and 2013 (Figure 5.3). The decline among states is due to the so-called BRICS effect: the emerging countries designated by this acronym (Brazil, Russia, India, China, and South Africa) are gradually catching up with developed countries. Chinese averages are now approaching European and North American levels, which themselves are rising less rapidly than in the past because of slowing growth and efforts to improve energy efficiency. At the same time, however, income inequality for the period increased within countries, which led to a rise in household CO_2e

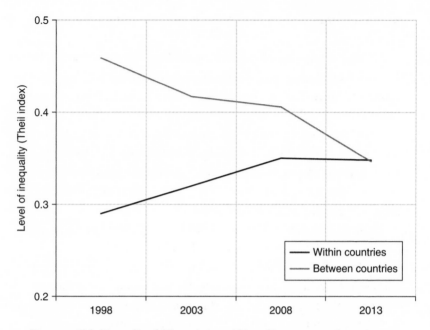

Figure 5.3. Global inequality of CO_2e emissions within and between countries, 1998–2013. Within countries carbon inequality increased between 1998 and 2013, while between countries inequality decreased. *Sources and series:* www.lucaschancel.info/hup.

emissions inequality. In 1998, only a third of world CO_2e emissions inequality was due to inequality within countries, compared to half today. This initial finding underscores the importance of ignoring national boundaries in seeking to allocate shares of responsibility for climate change.

The second striking result is that growth in CO_2e emissions was very unequally distributed within segments of the world's population during the fifteen years from 1998 to 2013. Figure 5.4 shows the increase in emissions for different income groups on a global scale. We began by classifying the world's population in 1998 in terms of individual emissions, going from the lowest emitter to the highest. Then we divided this population into fifty groups and measured the growth of average individual emissions within each of these groups for the entire period.

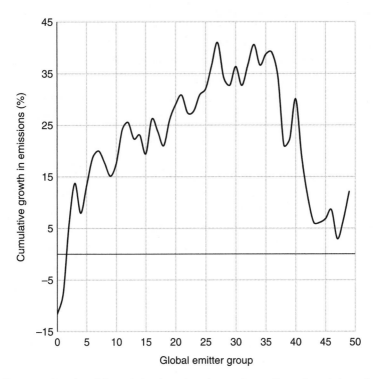

Figure 5.4. Growth in CO$_2$e emissions by emitter class, 1998–2013. Per capita emissions of the world's bottom 2 percent of emitters (Group 0 on the x-axis) fell by 12 percent between 1998 and 2013; in contrast, among the top 2 percent (Group 49 on the x-axis), they increased by 13.5 percent. *Sources and series:* www.lucaschancel.info/hup.

Emissions fell for income classes at the very bottom of the energy consumption scale: the poorest people in poor countries saw their emissions decline, a consequence of wars and unfavorable economic policies. Above them, emissions increased more and more strongly for all individuals situated below the highest 25 percent: the middle and upper classes in emerging countries benefitted from policies aimed at opening up national economies to world trade, enriching them and at the same time increasing their emission levels. The increase in emissions then very sharply declined above the thirty-fifth group, that is, for the upper 30 percent of emitters. This group corresponds mainly to the population of industrialized countries, which, under the dual influence of economic crisis and increased energy efficiency, saw their emissions grow at a relatively moderate rate. Near the top of the scale the curve flattens out, but then suddenly rises again for individuals at the very top: the wealthiest saw both their incomes and emissions strongly climb—but this in countries where emissions grew slowly, moderating the observed rise.

The third striking result is that despite the strides made by middle and upper classes in developing countries in catching up with their counterparts in developed countries, CO_2e emissions remain very highly concentrated at the global level. The overall per capita average is 6.2 metric tons; the top 10 percent emit on average twenty-eight metric tons and are responsible for about 45 percent of all emissions, whereas the bottom 50 percent (1.6 metric tons on average) are responsible for only about 13 percent of this pollution (Figure 5.5). In 2013, of the most polluting 10 percent of the world's population, a third came from emerging countries. While this lends support to the "hiding behind the poor" thesis, it also shows that the industrialized countries cannot be absolved of responsibility, since they still account for two-thirds of all emissions within this group.

This way of representing world CO_2e emissions inequality raises an important political question: can the responsibility of different social groups be addressed within an international framework based on a principle of multilateral negotiation among sovereign states? Evidently this is not a simple matter, but we will see in Part Three that there are several promising ways of bringing these results to the attention of climate negotiators.

In Part Two we have briefly considered three forms of environmental inequality: access to natural resources, exposure to risks, and responsi-

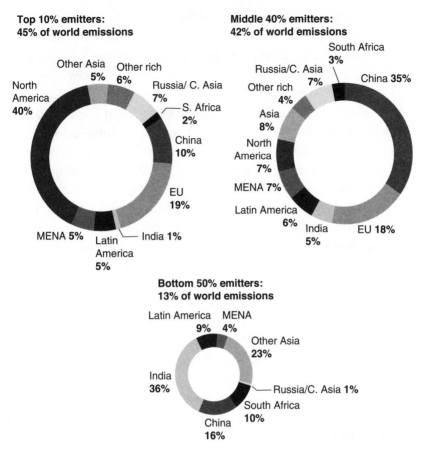

Figure 5.5. Global inequality of CO$_2$e emissions among individuals, 2013. The top 10 percent of emitters worldwide account for 45 percent of total emissions. Within this group, 40 percent of CO$_2$ emissions satisfy the needs of North Americans, 19 percent those of Europeans, and 10 percent those of Chinese. *Sources and series:* www.lucaschancel .info/hup.

bility for environmental degradation. Two main points need to be kept in mind.

First, economic inequalities determine environmental inequalities to a large extent: the poorest have a harder time, by definition, in gaining access to marketable natural resources (such as energy), but they also are more exposed to environmental risks and, as a result, are always more vulnerable to injury. Moreover, economic inequalities are the principal determinant of inequalities in greenhouse gas emissions. A sustained upward trend in economic imbalances therefore holds out little promise for reducing environmental injustice in the years ahead.

Second, environmental inequalities aggravate existing economic and social inequalities. Unequal access to limited quantities of energy has a negative impact on mental and physical development as well as on educational opportunity. Unequal exposure to the effects of pollution and other sources of environmental damage perpetuates and accentuates these same disadvantages, in industrialized and emerging countries alike.

It is therefore necessary to reduce economic inequalities while at the same time taking steps to protect the environment, without sacrificing the attainment of one objective for the other. The problem is that environmental protection can assume several forms, and not all of them are neutral with regard to economic inequality; some environmental policies can actually strengthen existing social and economic inequalities, at least for a certain time. As for policies aimed at narrowing differences in wealth, they may in their turn have undesirable consequences for the environment. Can a way be found to reconcile these two urgent imperatives?

PART THREE

Political, Social, and Economic
Policy Implications

6

Reducing Inequalities
in a Finite World

IN PARTS ONE AND TWO we have tried to identify the mechanisms that link economic and environmental inequalities with sustainable development. What we now need to consider is how the challenges presented by the many ways in which these various forms of inequality interact with one another can be most effectively met. A comprehensive answer is beyond the scope of this work. I will therefore content myself with laying out three major public policy initiatives with a view to advancing public debate on these questions.

First, substantial investments in energy, water, and public transport infrastructure will be needed—and they will also need to be accompanied by measures aimed at inculcating new norms of well-being through heightened public awareness, early education, and economic incentives. Second, these measures should be financed in part by ecological taxation, which, when it is well crafted, can be a powerful tool for reducing inequality and protecting the environment. Third, publicly transparent methods of analysis and accounting for measuring progress toward the reduction of environmental inequalities will need to be devised so that they may take their rightful place at the heart of public debate.

Before I take up these points in turn, let us consider the bell-shaped curve in Figure 5.4, which testifies to the emergence of a global middle class. From the economic point of view, this is rather good news: in emerging and developing countries, many more people are now able to enjoy a decent standard of living. From an environmental point of view, however, the curve is simply frightening: it means that the middle classes in these countries are catching up at the planet's expense.

Yet the fact that reducing inequalities within countries has grave implications for the earth's climate is not unanimously admitted, even among experts. Homi Kharas, director of the Global Economy and Development Program at the Brookings Institution in Washington, argues that the escape from poverty now being witnessed in much of the world does not increase global carbon emissions.[1] Kharas maintains that the poorest people in developing countries are responsible for more pollution than the lower middle classes. Why? Because the methods employed by peasant farmers in these countries are very unproductive and high in greenhouse gases emissions. This way of thinking reflects the enduring influence of the environmental Kuznets curve. And yet the studies we examined earlier are unequivocal: when the whole of per capita CO_2e emissions (domestic and foreign) are taken into account, the level of pollution increases with the standard of living—in Africa, in Europe, and in America. Other experts maintain that a more egalitarian distribution of income in a country such as the United States would automatically reduce national CO_2e emissions.[2] This is true only under certain conditions, however, that turn out not to be satisfied in practice.[3] In fact, income redistribution—other things being equal—tends to increase total emissions. That said, absolutely nothing prevents governments from acting in such a way that other things will not be equal. Household energy refurbishment targeted at low-income groups is one of the most promising options. A complementary approach is to tackle economic inequalities through traditional public policy measures (strengthening the social state and making taxation more progressive, for instance) while at the same time attempting to reduce environmental inequalities through measures that do not target a specific segment of the population (via environmental regulations or investments that do not favor specific social groups).

Reducing Inequalities by Minimizing Ecological Impact

Among the various tools available to decision makers for reducing inequalities, which ones are the most promising from the point of view of making the transition to an ecologically sustainable economy? Further empirical research and quantitative analysis will be needed to give a satisfactory answer, but we already know enough to be able to point public policy in the right direction.

For most people in emerging countries and for low-income persons in rich countries, strengthening public services is a way of tangibly improving living conditions while protecting the environment. This is true particularly when one considers energy grids, water distribution and purification systems, and public transportation networks.

PUBLIC SERVICES AND ENERGY COOPERATIVES

The case of Sweden is instructive in this regard. Beginning in the 1970s, the government launched a large-scale program for developing urban heat-distribution networks powered by renewable energy sources. This made it possible to reduce household energy consumption and associated CO_2e emissions, because district heating systems are more efficient than individual heating systems. Moreover, when energy costs increased following the introduction of a carbon tax in Sweden in the early 1990s, the existence of these networks permitted people to easily switch energy sources, thereby avoiding financial hardship. The primary beneficiaries of this program were the poorest, since the share of their household budgets devoted to energy was larger than that of those who were better off.

Today, three-quarters of the heat distributed by district systems in Sweden is supplied by renewable energy (or by recycled waste), and the systems are owned and administered by local public agencies. Massive investments over the past few decades have resulted in lower energy bills for all citizens, beginning with the least well-off, while at the same time helping to combat climate change.

Such investments have the further consequence of helping to slow the decline of public wealth that we noted in Chapter 2, and therefore of moderating the return to extremely high levels of highly concentrated private wealth observed since the 1980s. We should keep in mind that an increase in the amount of private capital is not a bad thing in itself. But because it has been accompanied in recent years by a marked increase in the concentration of inherited personal wealth, it raises concerns about the equitable sharing of wealth in a society and the rate at which estates are presently taxed.

Novel forms of private ownership of energy and environmental infrastructure may be imagined that would promote a more equitable distribution of wealth. In Germany, for example, significant volumes of investment have been made in decentralized infrastructure for energy production.[4] A good many private individuals have invested in utility cooperatives for the generation and transmission of electricity and heat, which is to say community-managed organizations whose members jointly own wind turbines, solar panels, and power plants for transforming biomass into electricity and also supervise the distribution of this energy to customers. As the transition to renewable energy sources gains momentum, the value of these investments will grow.

The governance model adopted by German energy cooperatives is exemplary from the point of view of social equity, since strategic decisions are made in accordance with the principle of one member, one vote—as opposed to the traditional model of investor-owned utilities where individual decision-making authority depends on the number of shares held. Moreover, the relatively low membership fees for energy cooperatives, typically €100 (not quite $115) per year, give broad scope for citizen involvement.

The experiment has been a success. Almost half of new renewable-energy power stations built in Germany since 2000 are run by private citizens (many of them small farmers) who have entered into cooperative arrangements, whereas the share of new facilities attributable to traditional energy utilities is only 7 percent. Energy cooperatives are by no means limited to local projects undertaken by a few neighbors sharing a solar roof; the largest German cooperative numbers some thirty-eight thousand members and distributes electricity to thirty-four thousand customers. Overall, German citizens have invested some €20 billion in such ventures since the turn of the century. The cooperative model has therefore proved to be scalable.

What explains the model's success? Its popularity among ordinary Germans certainly counts for a great deal (cooperatives operate in all sectors of the economy, and a quarter of the population belongs to one or another of them), but support from public authorities has played a crucial role as well, by making loans to citizen groups at preferential rates and by guaranteeing a stable financial and regulatory environment that encourages renewable-energy production under private sponsorship.

PUBLIC WATER UTILITIES

Water purification and distribution networks are another essential element of efforts to protect the environment and reduce inequality. Historically, responsibility for the distribution of water in North America and Europe was first assumed by private entities. These enterprises were unable to guarantee universal access to safe drinking water, however, and during the second half of the nineteenth century, a period of rapid industrialization and urbanization, cholera epidemics were frequent. Private companies were eventually replaced by public utilities, operating in most cases under municipal authority. In the United States, the New Deal put the private water sector out of business: by the late 1930s, virtually the whole of the nation's water distribution network had been made public, making it possible to extend coverage to the entire population while also putting an end to epidemics.

Still today, about 90 percent of American towns and cities are responsible for water supply systems and treatment facilities; waste disposal is typically managed by a public agency as well. The same pattern is observed in a majority of rich countries: more than 80 percent of their populations drink water distributed by a public operator. While claims regarding the efficiency of public water agencies have been challenged in recent decades, lending popular support for legislation aimed at encouraging the privatization of these and other services, public ownership remains very largely the norm.

What accounts for the preference in rich countries for public rather than private management of the water supply? Standard economic theory provides us with the answer in this case: where a natural monopoly exists, introducing competition has the effect of increasing costs rather than reducing them (it would make no sense, for example, to build two parallel water-supply networks); furthermore, theories of property rights and transaction costs tell us that private management of a natural monopoly of this kind requires a high level of supervision on the part of public authorities, particularly in order to prevent the private operator from extracting monopoly rents, and that this supervision can prove to be very costly.

As an empirical matter, it turns out that a good number of municipalities in the United States that opted for privatization in recent decades have since reverted to public management, because the quality of service under private management declined without the costs to consumers being lowered.[5] The first victims were the least well-off, who could not afford preferable alternatives (buying mineral water, for example).

In low-income countries, where government agencies responsible for monitoring water supply and waste treatment have yet to be established for the most part, universal public access to potable water is far from assured. Since the 1980s, a time when the ideology of privatization was ascendant, and as a consequence of the demonstrated incapacity of the public authorities, publicly managed water systems have been widely disparaged. In the intervening decades, emboldened by the warm reception given to their criticisms of the public sector, development banks have supported the privatization of water-supply networks in the developing world, with multinational corporations (notably among them two French water-management companies, Suez and Véolia) carving out for themselves the lion's share of the market. But these private entities have not always lived up to their responsibilities, especially with regard to quality of service and meeting the needs of the least well-off.[6]

The experience of municipalities such as Porto Alegre and Recife in Brazil, as well as of cities in the state of Karnataka in India and in Ghana, shows that in fact there is no incompatibility in low-income countries between quality of service and local public management of the water supply. In these places, investment decisions are made by resource users, which should in principle provide a surer guarantee that issues of social justice will be taken into account. As a practical matter, significant progress in supplying service to all while keeping costs under control has in fact been made.

The success of communal water management in rich countries, together with these recent examples in developing and emerging countries, confirms that public water utilities are not only a viable option today but also a promising one in the years ahead, making it possible to unite quality of service and economic efficiency with truly democratic access to the most essential of all natural resources.

THE FUTURE OF TRANSPORTATION

Local authorities and national governments have every reason to invest in public transit (not only bus, subway, and train lines, but also carpooling), again as a way of protecting the environment while achieving the aims of social policy. This is especially true in emerging countries. Consider the situation of a worker living in a suburb of New Delhi who works nine hours a day and travels an hour and a half by bus to go to work in the morning and then another hour and a half to come back home in the evening. This is the daily experience of millions of people in the Indian capital and in many other cities around the world. Not only does the cost of public transportation represent a very considerable portion of a worker's income (equal to almost 25 percent of the minimum wage, according to a World Bank report), but the time spent in transit also amounts to a 25 percent tax on total daily work time (three unpaid hours out of twelve).[7] Adding the real cost of transportation to this virtual tax yields a "pretax tax" on labor of nearly 50 percent.

New Delhi today has nearly twenty-two million inhabitants and ten million motor vehicles, three million of them cars. Ten years from now the number of cars could well exceed ten million, according to some estimates. Large-scale investment in public transportation would not only make it possible to avoid a massive increase in automobile traffic, which would be disastrous for the environment, but it would also make it possible to reduce transportation costs for the middle class and for the least well-off. But investing in public transportation will not be enough.

Changing Social Norms

The car, like many goods and services having a large carbon imprint, is not just a means of transportation like any other; it is also a way of advertising a certain standard of living. One buys a vehicle for practical and economic reasons, but also very often to signal one's membership in a social class. The playwright Arthur Miller, in *Death of a Salesman* (1949), a story of the American Dream and its frustrations, grants quite a special importance to Willy Loman's car. Without it he could not do his job. But it is much more than this. It is also the incarnation of his dream of individual liberty, of freedom of movement and upward social mobility. At the end of the play, Willy crashes his car against a wall—figuratively, a wall of disillusionment.

Similarly, in developing countries, car ownership is seen as proof of membership in the middle class. As a matter of fact, because of the difficulties in estimating the size of this class, researchers have proposed using the number of people who have a car as a proxy.[8] The perceived link between social status and owning a vehicle is simply catastrophic from the point of view of the planet. Some idea of the scale of the problem can be had by considering that the amount of energy indirectly associated with the production of a single car is almost equivalent to the energy needed to make it run for almost fifty thousand miles, not an insignificant amount.

The attachment to private car ownership also limits the state's capacity to invest in public transportation, which is a key element in protecting the environment. If the middle class feels that public transportation is good only for the working class, it will be less inclined to approve its financing through taxes. Public authorities therefore have everything to gain by addressing social stereotypes about wealth and status in order to increase the use of low-carbon and low-cost public transport.

How can this be done? New Delhi, like Bombay, has a new subway system, though it is still thoroughly insufficient by comparison with the size of these two megalopolises. It was recently proposed that first-class compartments be introduced to attract wealthy riders, who today prefer to travel behind the tinted windows of their luxury four-wheel-drive city cars. Some commentators criticized this measure, not unreasonably, as an attempt to further expand the inequalities of Indian society, literally pushing them underground. Others saw it as an effective marketing strategy on behalf of the Metro: if public transportation were to be used by elites, the middle class would see that there is no need to have a car to be rich. From an environmental point of view, as we have seen, trying to modify how different social classes think about modes of transportation makes good sense. As a marketing strategy, it is by no means new. It was successfully used by Antoine-Auguste Parmentier, an agronomist allotted land by Louis XVI, in order to win wide acceptance for the potato in France in the late eighteenth century. Parmentier is said to have had his fields surrounded by armed guards during the day but not at night, so that the villagers, having been led to believe that potatoes were a delicacy reserved for members of the royal court, would be able to steal them under cover of darkness.

In the two Indian cities, well-planned advertising campaigns (pointing out the inconveniences of travel by car, for example, and the extra purchasing power gained from shifting to public transport) could help to change popular ideas of comfort, while expressly disclaiming any intention to reproduce existing social inequalities in another form. In New Delhi, the municipal transit authority finally decided against introducing first-class compartments, but the proposal is still under consideration in Bombay. The debate surrounding the measure has had the merit at least of questioning social norms and their environmental impacts.

The stigmatization of certain forms of transportation and energy use is evidently not a monopoly of low-income emerging countries. In many metropolitan areas in Europe and the United States, the most economical and ecologically the soundest option for commuters is car-pooling. Yet this strategy still suffers in many people's minds from the reputation of being used by people who cannot afford to pay their own way. In addition to underwriting the costs of urban planning needed to develop carpooling to its fullest potential, government at all levels will bear much of the responsibility for making this mode of transportation socially more attractive.

One sometimes hears public service announcements on the radio urging listeners to reduce their consumption of energy and water. This is all very well and good, but whatever impression they make is small by comparison with the enormous volume of paid advertising promoting environmentally harmful lifestyles. Messages aimed at persuading people to adopt sustainable modes of consumption could be made to reach very large audiences via television and social media, in parallel with basic education in public schools, beginning in the early grades. This represents a considerable challenge for public policy, which takes too little interest today in advertising and public communication generally, leaving the field open to private sector interests that cannot be expected to have the same concern for protecting the environment and furthering the cause of social justice.

THE ENERGY REVOLUTION IN HOUSING

Making energy-efficient improvements to houses and apartments in order to better insulate them against the cold of winter and the heat of summer is another way to reduce both the ecological footprint of individuals and household budgetary constraints. It is now generally agreed that upgrading energy efficiency has the best, or at least one of the best, cost-benefit ratios when it comes to reducing carbon emissions. The cheapest energy, as the familiar saying has it, is the energy we do not use. Governments have a particularly important role to play in this connection. Poor households would be the first to gain from thermal insulation were it not for the fact that, at a cost of $40,000 or more for a single apartment, they simply cannot afford it.

Putting energy-efficient retrofitting within the reach of the least well-off is a good example of effective social and ecological policy. It moderates energy consumption and eases budgetary constraints for beneficiaries, who find themselves better protected against rises in the price of gas, heating fuel, and electricity. How, then, can such investment be financed?

The obvious answer, or so it would appear, is to draw funds from general operating budgets. It is the state's responsibility, after all, to fund programs that will benefit the whole of society and future generations. France and Great Britain both grant means-tested assistance to poor households for energy-saving improvements. But the pace of renovation is still too slow to be effective on a large scale. A more promising alternative is an innovative method known as third-party financing, which allows households to undertake energy-saving improvements without having to advance any of their own money.

In the Paris region, for example, a consortium of public lenders (regional and municipal governments, and the state bank) enables individuals and families to pay for energy-saving improvements without having to spend any money up front. The underwriters are reimbursed over the long term through reductions in household consumption: households continue to pay the same energy bill as before, with the difference going to the lenders until the cost of the project has been entirely repaid. In the end, individuals benefit from improved thermal insulation and lower energy bills.

Many successful examples of third-party financing may be found in developing countries, which are often very much at the forefront in such matters. In Tunisia and India, for example, loan arrangements of this sort have been designed to permit low-income households, many of them unable to afford the initial costs of renewable energy technologies, to purchase more efficient appliances and to install solar panels.

CHANGING POPULAR ATTITUDES ABOUT ENERGY USE

In the case of energy-saving improvements, many studies have disclosed the existence of a counterintuitive rebound effect: energy consumption increases when normally it would have been expected to decrease. The level of heat thought to be comfortable increases with the quality of the heating system, so that after thermal retrofitting, in a country such as France, 30 percent of the anticipated savings are not realized.[9] For families living in dilapidated housing, of course, their homes are bound to seem more agreeable than they used to. But because temperature settings are nonetheless often higher than what is generally accepted to be reasonable for a healthy person, it will be necessary to educate beneficiaries of public assistance about appropriate levels of usage so that thermal renovation brings about a real change in consumption habits.

In countries where social protection systems are well established, however, social workers' understanding of the ecological aspects of sustainable development is usually very limited, and, conversely, technocrats responsible for planning the energy / ecological transition know little about its social implications. Timothée Erard, Mathieu Saujot, and I have shown in a study that this is one of the major problems in combating energy insecurity today.[10] The social-ecological state of the twenty-first century must therefore develop synergies (of policy implementation, information sharing, and training) among the various ministries and branches of administration (environment and energy, social affairs, employment, and budget).[11]

Such an approach would gain in effectiveness if it were to be extended beyond the field of thermal renovation to include broader access to low-carbon transportation and advice concerning healthier diets. Again, it will be instructive to look to northern Europe for inspiration. In Sweden, for example, the calculation of social assistance provided to individuals takes into account their energy expenditures so that those who live on very tight budgets receive more than others. Individuals are encouraged to seek guidance from social workers who are trained to evaluate the amount of energy they consume in connection with housing, transportation, and so forth, with a view to taking this information into consideration in calculating the overall level of public assistance for which financially insecure households are eligible.[12] In Germany, energy subsidies are likewise included in reckoning the amount of social assistance to be given to the unemployed. The mechanisms of social security in both Germany and Sweden incorporate the energy dimension among the various risks that individuals incur in the course of their lives.

A Green New Deal Is Good for Jobs

So far we have identified several areas—affordable energy, clean water, improved sanitation, low-carbon transportation—in which the active participation of public authorities is essential both in protecting the environment and guaranteeing universal access to these resources. It is a reason for optimism that targeted policies have proved to be perfectly viable from the point of view of economic efficiency. What is more, investment in energy infrastructure is labor-intensive. Various studies have shown that a dollar invested in the thermal renovation of housing units or the construction of public transportation networks will create more jobs than a dollar invested in most other sectors.[13] Ecological transition investments in general are labor-intensive. The jobs they create—many of them well-paid manufacturing and engineering jobs—cannot be sent abroad, unlike many other jobs in the service sector today.

This is the rationale behind the Green New Deal advocated by Representative Alexandria Ocasio-Cortez in the United States, and by others in Europe over the past decade. Investing now in large-scale ecological transition investments is not only good (and, in fact, necessary) for the planet. It is also just good economics.

It is true that certain sectors of the economy (such as coal mining or the oil industry) will be negatively affected by a Green New Deal. But this is precisely the point: transforming an economy's production structure will help to preserve the environment and protect public health. The decision to invest in certain sectors while regulating others more heavily to preserve national interests has many precedents in the history of market democracies, and not solely in wartime. In the 1960s, the French government made massive investments in nuclear power, lowering production in other electricity-generating sectors of the economy (coal, oil, and gas, for instance). More recently, when the United States signed the Montreal Protocol in 1987 to ban the use of gases responsible for ozone layer depletion, this inevitably had an adverse impact on the producers of such gases.

The basic idea of a Green New Deal is that it is both possible and desirable to protect workers' health while letting certain polluting industries transform or eventually close. What matters is the welfare of human beings, not of firms. That said, it should be noted that cleaning up mining facilities (and nuclear sites) requires technical expertise and experience that workers in these sectors already possess to one degree or another. The old polluting industries are singularly well equipped to lead the way in repairing environmental damage for the decades to come, which is another effective way to protect employment in these sectors. Moreover, in cases where the skills of the workers in polluting sectors cannot be used for ecological transition purposes, social policies can and should be designed to provide training and financial support for both individuals and communities.

Progressive Ecological Taxation

How are policies that are crucial to bringing about the social and ecological transition to be financed? Taxation, though it is often maligned today, nonetheless fulfills three important functions: it collects the money needed for the delivery of public services, corrects market inequalities, and modifies behavior (by deterring people from contributing to pollution, for example). The third function is thought by many to be objectionable: taxes, it is held, make markets inefficient (by discouraging hiring, reducing investment, and so on). John Maynard Keynes's teacher, Arthur Cecil Pigou, long ago turned the argument of opponents of taxation against them by demonstrating that modifying behaviors is not the least important of the effects that a tax on labor or capital should seek to bring about.[14] Reducing incentives to pollute—the behavior that interests us here—while at the same time diminishing inequalities is not easily done, but it is possible.

Let us look once more at the example of New Delhi and its three million cars, a figure expected to increase by a factor of three in the next ten years. Taxing individual car owners—by means of annual vehicle inspection, for example—would be a progressive measure since it targets the wealthiest 15 percent or so of the population. In ten years, however, car ownership will have been largely democratized. The tax base will be much larger, but the tax itself will be significantly less progressive. Developing countries therefore have an opportunity in the next few years to put into place progressive tax measures having a substantial environmental effect—and one that will be all the greater as the funds raised in this way can be used to improve public transportation. Once the window has closed, the measure will no longer be as socially just, and, if nothing has been done in the meantime to provide an alternative model, the norm of individual car ownership will be an integral part of the consumption habits of the new middle class.

The idea of a carbon tax has gained support in many countries, but there is still a long way to go. Worldwide, favorable tax treatment and direct fuel subsidies (to kerosene users, for example) cost governments more than $300 billion each year.[15] In developing countries, these subsidies are often described as a form of assistance for poor households. In reality, however, as the Swedish economist Thomas Sterner has shown, they benefit mainly the urban rich.[16] Poor households do, of course, profit from lower prices for kerosene and gasoline, which they use for lighting and cooking—a very considerable benefit considering how little money they have even to pay for necessities. But by far the larger part of these subsidized savings end up in the pockets of those who consume many more petroleum products in order to drive their cars and run their air conditioning and heating systems. The wealthiest 20 percent of developing countries benefit six times more from pollution subsidies than do the poorest 20 percent.

Eliminating these subsidies (and raising tax rates) therefore frees up substantial sums for public expenditures. Only a few years ago in Indonesia, for example, fossil fuel subsidies amounted to a quarter of the government's budget; in 2012, they were three times greater than the whole of government spending on health and social protection.[17] These were funds that could be reserved more specifically for poor families or for the development of social security programs once the subsidies were repealed.

In Iran, the authorities canceled gasoline subsidies and redirected half of the savings to households, opening a bank account for every family that applied for assistance. In Indonesia, successive reductions in fuel subsidies in recent years made it possible to fund health insurance, education investments, and social assistance programs for the neediest. Such expenditures grew by about the same amount that fossil fuel subsidies were reduced. Here is an example of a progressive reform that consolidates a vast system of universal social security (one of the most comprehensive in the world) while at the same time creating a powerful disincentive in relation to fossil fuel use. What we are witnessing in both of these countries is the emergence of a social/ecological state.

Environmental tax reforms that represent social progress rather than retreat can be carried out in rich countries as well. They have a greater chance of winning political acceptance if they are incorporated in a larger program of tax reform that allows the losers from such reforms to be better compensated.[18] Recent research shows that a carbon tax without any compensatory mechanism is regressive in rich countries (it weighs more heavily upon the poor as a proportion of income), but it may become progressive if it is accompanied by targeted transfers to low-income households, whether directly or indirectly (through a reduction in social security contributions for low earners, for example).

More or less successful examples of environmental tax reform may be found in Europe and elsewhere. The pioneering Swedish measure was introduced almost thirty years ago as part of a comprehensive tax reform package aimed not only at instituting a carbon tax but also at modernizing the nation's tax system. The tax on carbon emissions went from €27 per metric ton in 1991 to €120 per metric ton today, one of the highest rates in the world. It needs to be kept in mind, however, that the price of reform was reducing marginal tax rates for the wealthiest, a concession to political reality that undermined the new system's claim to be progressive. The increase in carbon tax rates was nonetheless accompanied by large-scale public investments in low-carbon energy infrastructures, which provided taxpayers with alternatives when emissions reached high levels. The Swedish system also offers tailored social security support to individuals with high energy bills, which is critical to ensure that carbon taxation does not hurt the poor.

Lessons from the Yellow Vests
Movement in France

Earlier, in Chapter 2, I mentioned the French government's attempt to introduce a carbon tax in 2008. Policymakers from both the left and the right opposed the measure on the ground that it was antisocial, and it was rejected before it could be implemented.

In 2014, the center-left government finally managed to win legislative approval for a carbon tax. How did it manage to succeed where another government had failed only a few years before? The new tax bill established rates at almost zero euros per metric ton of carbon emitted the first year, with the result that barely anyone noticed the new tax. Energy experts and environmentalists praised the political genius of the government and looked forward to the steady increases contemplated by the schedule of tax rates in the years ahead.

Few expected the social unrest that was about to come.[19] Because the planned rise in carbon tax revenues had not been accompanied either by additional compensatory mechanisms to offset the burden on low- and middle-income households or by a significant increase in energy transition investments, however, millions of households had no low-carbon transport or heating alternatives. In the absence of any meaningful financial assistance, rising carbon tax rates were bound to trigger popular discontent.

This is what finally happened in 2018, when the new center-right government of Emmanuel Macron ratcheted up the carbon tax as part of a broader plan to scrap the wealth tax and reduce tax rates on capital incomes. Taxes on the richest of the rich were reduced by more than €4 billion that year, while carbon tax revenues, raised disproportionately from low- and middle-income households, were increased by about €4 billion.

In the event, the government's claim that the tax deal would be proclimate and propoor was contradicted by the numbers: while the richest 1 percent saw their incomes increase by more than 6 percent thanks to the reform (and up to 20 percent for the top 0.1 percent of earners), the bottom 20 percent of households were actually net losers in the tax overhaul, mainly because of the increase in carbon tax rates.[20] Under these circumstances (worsened by a rise in global oil and gas energy prices), low- and middle-income taxpayers felt justified in arguing that they were, in effect, subsidizing tax cuts that benefited the wealthiest—a charge that, everything considered, was not unjust. The fact of the matter is that less than 10 percent of the tax revenue was dedicated to helping people in the middle and at the bottom, so the rest did indeed amount to a massive tax gift for the very rich.

In the wake of a petition to freeze the carbon tax, an unprecedented social movement quickly took shape, assuming the form of nationwide protests that came to dominate the government's agenda for months. Social justice was one of the movement's chief concerns. Many protesters also denounced the absence of taxation on kerosene-based aviation fuel (stigmatized as a "fuel for the rich") while they had to pay taxes at the gas station. Here again the protesters had a point: someone driving to work every day was obliged to pay the carbon tax, but someone flying from Paris to the south of France for the weekend did not have to pay any tax on fuel.

The lack of compensatory mechanisms and the widespread sense of injustice led to a politically tense situation that eventually compelled the government to freeze the carbon tax. The French example might usefully serve as a case study of how not to reform taxation in the twenty-first century. If governments do not develop comprehensive programs that will help working-class households adapt to new tax and regulatory environments and ensure that all social groups contribute their fair share to energy transition efforts, environmental policies are likely to be opposed, sometimes by violent means.

The reality is that there are other courses of action available to us. In Indonesia, as we have seen, an adroit combination of energy price increases and investments in social security made it possible to secure public support for the measure—the opposite of what happened in

France in 2018. The Canadian province of British Columbia, which introduced a carbon levy in January 2008, more recently moved to compensate the working and middle classes by giving back more than a quarter of the receipts to households in the form of payments whose amount is progressively calculated: reimbursement diminishes as the level of income rises.

Measuring Environmental Inequalities

In Part Two, we saw that not everyone is equally vulnerable in the face of environmental risks and shocks. Public policy must therefore also devise ways of reducing inequalities of access and exposure. Damien Demailly, Felix Sieker, and I have shown that these forms of inequality have not yet really made it onto government agendas, particularly in Europe.[21] This is due chiefly to the fact that they have not been adequately measured: without a satisfactory system of evaluation, these inequalities will not be able to find their proper place in international debate and negotiation, and therefore will not receive the consideration they deserve. The main thing that needs to be done today, then, is to develop methods for measuring environmental injustice that are both reliable and freely accessible.

Let us come back to the report that Thomas Piketty and I published on the eve of the Conference of the Parties (COP) 21 conference in 2015 on inequalities in global greenhouse gas emissions.[22] The question of responsibility for indirect emissions (pollution from foreign manufacturing that satisfies our domestic needs) is not addressed in official climate negotiations. Geopolitical considerations are part of the reason for this (European countries and the United States will have to make a greater financial commitment if emissions produced in China to meet Western demand are taken into account), but it is due also to the fact that until recently there was no way of accurately measuring imported emissions.

Measurement is never neutral: it is a political act—which nonetheless does not necessarily mean a partisan act, or a means of gaining tactical advantage. Nor is accurately measuring an inequality a sufficient condition for remedying it; with regard to income inequality, for example, reliable measures have been available for several years now, but still inequality continues to increase. Nevertheless it is a crucial step in making issues of this kind matter for international deliberation and action.

Certain countries lead the way and others clearly lag behind. Surprisingly, perhaps, government agencies and researchers in the United States stand out from the rest. The ambitious programs they have inaugurated for the purpose of measuring and mapping environmental injustices are responsible in large part for very active movements on behalf of environmental justice and against environmental racism that, since the early 1980s, have forced public agencies to collect, organize, and publish such information.

I will limit myself here to mentioning two important initiatives in the United States, which established it as a leader in the tracking of environmental inequalities until President Donald Trump set about dismantling environmental protection programs and agencies. The first initiative, the National Environmental Public Health Tracking Network, launched in 2005, was intended to bring together researchers in a number of fields with the common purpose of facilitating the collection, exchange, monitoring, analysis, and dissemination of data relating to public health and environmental inequalities. Its sponsors include the Centers for Disease Control and Prevention (CDC), the National Aeronautics and Space Administration (NASA), and the Environmental Protection Agency (EPA). Collaboration among different disciplines and agencies is absolutely crucial if environmental science is to meet the challenges facing us.

The second is an internet platform created by the EPA for its risk screening environmental indicators (RSEI) model, which allows the general public to monitor exposure to more than three hundred air and water pollutants at the local level. The usefulness of such a model is twofold: it permits citizens to become aware of the injustices to which they are subject and therefore to plead their case before government agencies and the courts, while also enabling public health and other officials to have a better sense of problems urgently needing to be addressed. Moreover, state and local agencies can plug their own data into the RSEI and, by extrapolating to a national scale, obtain information that the federal government itself does not yet have. It is disheartening, to say the least, to observe the systematic attempts by the climate skeptics who currently hold power in the United States to dismantle the EPA, perhaps the greatest force for good in research on the environment there is today.

The platform put in place by the EPA is unrivaled in its scope and transparency. It has no equivalent anywhere else in the world, not at the level of national analysis, nor with regard to the degree of detail in which pollution can be studied. A platform for measuring and mapping environmental inequalities at the local and national levels has been developed in France, for example, a complex undertaking that required data relating to public health, industrial production, socioeconomic patterns of consumption, and geographic distributions to be collected and cross-checked on a fine scale (on the order of a square kilometer). As one recent report points out, it is extremely problematic under French law, as under the law of many countries, to use data for a purpose other than the one for which they were produced.[23] This is a good thing from the point of view of protecting individual privacy, but it complicates the work of many researchers in this field, who are no less capable of preserving the anonymity of data than are medical researchers.[24]

The French platform is a first step toward properly measuring inequalities of exposure, but it is still very far from achieving as fine-grained a picture of environmental inequalities as in the United

States; by the end of 2016, exposure to only four pollutants had been measured and mapped. Furthermore, it is not enough to create such a platform. A place has to be created for it in the political landscape as well. For the moment, the platform is not accessible to all online. Transparency, as in the United States, is necessary if citizens are to be able to make these issues their own and to make their voices heard in public debate. Finally, because environmental pollution knows no geographic or political boundaries, it is essential that tools be developed on a transnational (in this case, European) level. When it comes to environmental inequalities, as with so many other things, open access to data on as large a scale as possible is indispensable if watchdog groups are to be able to demand public accountability and meaningful reform is to be achieved.

Financing Reductions in Environmental Inequalities

Reducing environmental inequalities inevitably entails costs, but these must be balanced against the ones they make it possible to avoid. The costs associated with premature births due to pollution amount to more than $5 billion a year in the United States alone.[25] In France, according to the Environment Ministry, the sum total of costs associated with pollution (including various types of illness and impacts on productivity) may be expected to rise by between €20 billion and €30 billion per year—as much money as could be saved if pollution were to be brought under control.[26] It goes without saying, of course, that calculating the value of protecting health and human life is not a matter that can be left to accountants. Nevertheless there is no getting around the need to accurately estimate environmental costs. In the event that these costs cannot be fully reimbursed by the benefits they produce, innovative methods of financing of the sort we looked at earlier will need to be called upon to make up the difference.

In our study on carbon and inequality, Piketty and I proposed financing the adaptation to climate change through a progressive tax on greenhouse gas emissions.[27] This means that the financial contributions of polluters must increase with the level of pollution, as opposed to the carbon taxes currently being discussed in international forums, which set a fixed rate for all polluters. A measure of this sort would not take the place of a conventional carbon tax aimed at modifying polluters' behavior; instead, it would complement it.

We adopted a global perspective: how is humanity to find the €150 billion (about $170 billion) that will be needed annually if those who are most vulnerable to the effects of climate change throughout the world are to be able to adapt? We proposed several strategies for progressive taxation of individual emissions (one in which funding comes from a tax on all those whose emissions are above the average, another in which the top 10 percent of emitters are taxed, and a third in which the top 1 percent is taxed) and examined the geographic patterns of distribution each one would imply (see Table 6.1). We found that, if the tax burden were to be proportionally shared by the top 10 percent of emitters, about 46 percent of the total contribution would come from North America, 16 percent from Europe, and 12 percent from China.

The specific problem we were trying to solve was how to finance the adaptation to climate change in developing countries, but a similar scheme for financing the reduction in inequalities of exposure in industrialized countries can easily be imagined. The principle is simple: the contribution of polluters must sharply increase with the level of pollution, by analogy with a progressive tax on income. Ideally, one would have detailed information concerning the amount of pollution, both direct and indirect, attributable to each person's level of energy consumption. This is not possible today, but it may be possible a few years from now thanks to recent advances in devising methods and tools for measuring per capita emissions. In the meantime a progressive tax could be instituted on levels of consumption that are relatively

Table 6.1. A progressive tax on global CO_2e emissions

| Region | Financing in proportion to total emissions (proportional tax on CO_2e) | Financing by progressive taxes on CO_2e | | | Financing by a tax on airline tickets (%) |
		Strategy 1 Share of financing among all emitters above the world average (%)	Strategy 2 Share of financing among top 10% of emitters (2.3 times the world average) (%)	Strategy 3 Share of financing among top 1% of emitters (9.1 times the world average) (%)	
North America	21.2	35.7	46.2	57.3	29.1
European Union	16.4	20.0	15.6	14.8	21.9
China	21.5	15.1	11.6	5.7	13.6
Russia / Central Asia	6.0	6.6	6.3	6.1	2.8
Other OECD countries	4.6	5.8	4.5	3.8	3.8
Middle East / North Africa	5.8	5.4	5.5	6.6	5.7
Latin America	5.9	4.3	4.1	1.9	7.0
India	7.2	1.0	0.7	0.0	2.9
Other Asian countries	8.3	4.7	4.1	2.7	12.1
Sub-Saharan Africa	3.1	1.5	1.5	1.1	1.1
World	100.0	100.0	100.0	100.0	100.0

Note: The table shows the share of emissions emitted by different groups in large world regions and the share of a global progressive carbon tax they would have to pay under different tax schemes. Source: Chancel and Piketty (2015).

easy to estimate (energy used for heating, for example, or for commuting to work). The principle of a progressive levy (the more one consumes, the higher the unit tax) already exists in many towns in France for water and waste disposal, and in some countries and US states for energy (Italy and California), but it has not yet explicitly been discussed in the case of carbon emissions.

Another option is to tax consumer goods that may reasonably be considered proxies for both a high standard of living and a high level of CO_2e emissions. A very modest per capita levy on airline tickets already exists in a dozen African countries and in France; the revenue is mostly used for the purpose of funding UNITAID, an international drug purchasing facility that fights pandemics (HIV / AIDS, tuberculosis, malaria) in developing countries. This tax could be substantially increased (it amounts today to only €1.40 per ticket, less than $2) and extended to other countries. By raising the rate for first class and business class, it could be made a progressive tax as well. A levy of €20 on all economy-class tickets and €180 on first-class tickets, for example, would yield the required sum of €150 billion annually.

Finally—even if it would not, strictly speaking, be a progressive option—CO_2e emissions could be heavily taxed at a single rate and energy consumption vouchers issued on a means-tested basis; alternatively, transfers could be made through a broader program of tax reform, which brings us back to a topic we considered earlier. At all events there are several ways in which rates of taxation can be modulated as a function of a polluter's level of responsibility in order to finance the reduction of environmental inequalities on a worldwide basis.

It is quite possible, then, to narrow economic inequalities while taking environmental constraints into consideration. We have looked at three approaches: first, modernizing public transportation and energy and water supply systems, through new investments in infrastructure and support for households adapting to ecological transition, in order to accelerate the evolution of social norms; second, devising novel methods of ecological taxation, which, when they are well designed, can overcome political opposition to certain forms of environmental protection; and third, reducing environmental inequalities, which will require that European nations and developing countries, following the American example, establish open and transparent platforms for measuring inequalities. All these initiatives are feasible; indeed, they have already been undertaken in various countries. In combination, they can bring about a genuine transformation of public policy.

7

Local Organization vs. International Coordination

IN CHAPTER 6, WE TRIED to discover which public policies need to be put into effect in order to guarantee greater social justice while at the same time promoting sustainable development. In most cases, state agencies and regional councils must play a crucial role. But we saw that policy coordination with municipal authorities is also necessary, and not only with regard to social welfare. The question arises, then, whether political action should not be taken at other levels as well, either still more locally within countries (at the level of small cities and towns), or more broadly among countries (regionally and globally), or both. It will be plain from what follows that economic and environmental inequalities cannot be effectively addressed at any one level alone.

Social and Ecological Justice at the Community Level

A number of social movements led by Greens or anarchists, reacting against the slowness, and sometimes the incapacity, of states to act to address social and environmental inequalities and to commit themselves to advancing the cause of ecological transition, call for a local approach to problems of social justice that relies on bonds of interdependence among people in small communities, through sharing, gifts, and mutual aid. The Transition Town movement inaugurated in England by Rob Hopkins in 2005 and amplified with the founding two years later of the Transition Network, a charity devoted to supporting initiatives in some fifty countries, is particularly interesting in this regard. It brings together like-minded people who consider the ecological transition to be inevitable ("Either you prepare for it or you will suffer the consequences," as they say), and who are determined to take action on a local level.[1] The movement catalyzes initiatives such as sharing networks (donations, recycling, and so forth), energy cooperatives, and the use of local currencies in order to support small neighborhood shops and businesses. In addition to increasing access to energy, its followers work to clean up pollution sites and assist those who have lost their jobs.

The great strength of such citizen movements is that they draw upon shared resources and motivations, a sense of community, and a resolve to attack problems at their source, reinforcing a joint commitment to the common good.[2] This spirit of civic allegiance is a fine example of what Paul Ricoeur meant by sociability—a feeling of solidarity without which a society cannot long survive. For a society cannot simply guarantee access to a minimum of material resources; it must also satisfy a basic need for recognition by one's fellows.[3] Today, however, many taxpayers no longer feel that governments acknowledge their dignity as citizens, and they are less and less willing to acquiesce in their cold-blooded fiscal power. But even when people join together for the purpose of reducing inequalities and making the ideal of solidarity a reality in their communities, they cannot escape the need for a social state in solving the problems we have been considering. In the case of economic inequalities, although the mutual aid embodied by private associations provides a safety net and other forms of support for individuals recovering from economic or environmental shocks, local communities quickly find themselves at a loss to deal with situations involving monetary redistribution. Establishing a minimum wage, or preventing tax evasion, or halting the depletion of natural resources outside their borders requires concerted action on the national level, if not also on the international level.

With regard to environmental inequalities, local communities have an essential role to play in drawing official attention to problems and in putting policy strategies into effect. This is what decades of struggle against environmental racism and other injustices have shown, not only in the United States but throughout the world. Here again, however, responses cannot be solely local and community-based. To take only the example of climate change, remedying environmental inequalities on a piecemeal basis means abandoning the cause of putting an end to global warming; in order to effectively tackle this problem, industrial, trade, and transportation policies have to be co-ordinated on a vast scale, at both the national and international levels. Whether one likes it or not, atmospheric pollution and chemical con-tamination of soil and water go beyond local boundaries.

With regard to coping with the effects of environmental shocks, there is much that well-organized local communities can do in the way of advance planning and crisis management. The work of the environ-mental economist Edward Barbier in analyzing the systemic failures— failures of technology and politics alike—that led to catastrophes such as Hurricane Katrina has shown the crucial role of neighborhood as-sociations, community lobbying groups, and individual political ac-tivists in improving the resilience of populations and places: urgent tasks such as educating the public about life-saving precautionary mea-sures and organizing evacuations are often best carried out at the local level.[4] Here again, however, community action by itself is not enough. When damages are very considerable (the total cost of Katrina exceeded more than $100 billion), it is necessary to spread risk as widely as possible over space and time. This is exactly what the social state makes it possible to do.

Local communities therefore cannot replace the social state in man-aging economic and environmental inequalities. The two levels are complementary and noninterchangeable. Yet some local solidarity movements reject government intervention—sometimes for good reason, because the social state has not always kept its promises. As far as social and environmental justice are concerned, however, the absence of state participation would pose grave dangers. Some conservative politicians disagree, arguing that since localities have increasingly assumed responsibility in recent years for assuring social solidarity, the scope of public services can be reduced. This is what the former British prime minister David Cameron was telling voters during the 2010 general election when he proposed substituting "big society" for "big government." A more compelling case can be made that by relying on communities to create social bonds and give meaning once more to ideals of social solidarity, the social state stands to gain in power and legitimacy. But whether this will actually happen is far from clear. For the moment, as the French jurist Alain Supiot rightly observes, no one can say with confidence whether new forms of citizen cooperation will strengthen or weaken the social state in the years ahead.[5] The challenge facing both governments and communities is to work out how they can cooperate most effectively, in order not only to define the terms of their mutual dependence but also, in the case of governments, to prevent the instruments of social justice from being wrested from them by communities.

Here a parallel can be discerned with the establishment of health care facilities for the working classes in the late nineteenth and early twentieth centuries in France. Initially independent, these facilities were eventually integrated into the existing hospital system as functionally autonomous components, while nonetheless having the same mission as the public health service (and particularly the obligation to treat all patients equally, without discrimination). In a similar spirit, private associations and movements working for social and environmental justice that demonstrate respect for certain fundamental principles might reasonably look to governments for a share of their funding. Charitable contributions are tax-deductible in many countries. In the case of donations to organizations acting in the public interest, one could imagine the state adding a certain percentage. This is not a new idea. In England, for example, a donation of £100 to an organization whose civic value is officially recognized becomes enlarged by 25 percent, with the result that the organization receives £125 and the donor is entitled to claim £25 as a tax write-off.[6]

Beyond the Social State

Governments therefore face competition from below, at the local level, but they also face competition from above in the form of forces beyond their control—environmental problems and inequalities of income and inherited wealth that cannot be adequately dealt with within the restricted framework of the nation-state. Pollution crosses borders, no less than capital flows do. Without policy coordination on taxation, trade, and social protection, individual states simply do not have the tools or the critical mass necessary to reduce economic and ecological inequalities.

Alongside the various forms of grassroots action that have taken root in local communities, another, still embryonic, movement is taking shape that calls for issues of social and ecological justice to be managed on a worldwide basis. With regard to environmental issues, the ongoing series of climate conferences has affirmed the necessity of treating them in a coordinated manner on a global scale, frankly acknowledging the difficulties involved while at the same time displaying a collective resolve to move forward. The agreement reached at the Paris conference in December 2015 was historic—notwithstanding the announcement by the United States a year and a half later that it would withdraw from it after the 2020 presidential election. While the accord has by no means solved the climate problem (the most recent surveys indicate that most signatories have failed to meet the targets set for reducing greenhouse gas emissions), it nonetheless proves that international cooperation is still possible.[7]

With regard to economic inequalities, no such cooperation presently exists. But there are two recent developments that give reason for optimism. The first is the agreement by the member states of the United Nations, as part of the negotiations over sustainable development goals (SDGs) that I discussed in Chapter 1, on a common indicator for measuring changes in economic inequality within countries. The use of a shared metric in this connection is important for three reasons.

First, it serves to frame debate on both national and international levels, not least because it provides a common language for evaluating government action to reduce income inequalities in particular.

Next, the various local, national, and international actors mobilized in the fight against economic inequalities can use the metric as leverage for calling to account states that do not reach the objectives they have set for themselves. It amounts, then, to a novel means of exerting political pressure through international comparison. (This leverage can be powerful: one has only to consider the effect of the Organisation for Economic Co-operation and Development's Program for International Student Assessment [PISA] rankings on educational policies to be convinced of it; in Germany, for example, the educational system was restructured so that its fifteen-year-olds would not continue to be among the poorest-performing students in Europe.) One might reasonably have supposed that economic inequality, as only one among more than a hundred SDG indicators, would very quickly have been drowned in a sea of data and forgotten. But this turns out not to be the case at all—it is taken very seriously. In the wake of the Stiglitz Commission's report on new measures of progress, many countries (and regions) have adopted national performance indicators aimed at "going beyond GDP."[8] With regard to eighteen national or regional initiatives, three-quarters of the data sets include at least one indicator of economic inequality.[9]

Finally, at least in theory, the use of a common indicator for this purpose within the SDG framework does more than merely classify performance; it also encourages states to learn from their neighbors. Identifying who leads the way and who brings up the rear in reducing economic inequalities shines a light on those measures that work and those that are doomed to fail. Chile, under the presidency of Michelle Bachelet, succeeded in enacting a comprehensive tax reform package in September 2014. How could its neighbors fail to be inspired by it? More generally, how can European countries learn from the Chilean experience? For this to happen within the SDG framework, the worlds of research and civil society will have to take charge. In that case one might imagine a renewed spirit of cooperation bringing delegates around a table, under the eyes of international civil society, where they will tell each other exactly what their countries intend to do. This may seem improbable, but it is nonetheless what happened in the case of climate negotiations: twenty years ago, few people would have thought it possible. Already one observes positive developments with respect to inequalities. To name only one, the 2018 annual assembly of the Economic and Social Commission for Asia and the Pacific (ESCAP) (the largest of the United Nations member regions) was devoted to addressing inequalities, and member countries took turns laying out the policies that they were putting in place.[10]

In its present form, the SDG framework does not accommodate genuine policy coordination on taxation, trade, and financial flows. But there is another one that might. This is the second of the two developments I mentioned a moment ago. It involves the initiatives on tax transparency being pursued within the framework of the Global Forum on Tax Transparency and Exchange of Information for Tax Purposes, sponsored by the Group of Twenty (G20) and the Organisation for Economic Co-operation and Development (OECD), and, since April 2016, the Platform for Collaboration on Tax, sponsored by the World Bank, the International Monetary Fund, the OECD, and the United Nations. Between 2017 and 2018, more than a hundred countries agreed to exchange bank information, in many cases automatically. It must be admitted, however, that this development, positive though it undoubtedly is, is still far from doing all that needs to be done, largely because it approaches the matter in an overly sectorial way that fails to pay sufficient attention to its larger political aspects.

Unless tax havens can be threatened with commercial and financial reprisals in the event that they do not supply the required information, how will it be possible to bring pressure on governments that often can count on support from one or more of the major powers? So long as sanctions are not commensurate with the gains realized through fraud, the chances of real and lasting change are extremely small. The economist Gabriel Zucman has shown that France, Italy, and Germany will need to threaten Switzerland with a 30 percent tariff on exports if they seriously mean to discourage the Swiss from harboring tax evaders.[11]

Moreover, a variety of measures are available for combating certain types of tax evasion. Here I shall very briefly consider only one of them. Many states are victims today of tax optimization schemes (so-called legal tax evasion) employed by multinational corporations seeking to relocate a share of their profits in countries where the tax on corporate profits is low or actually zero. Their success so far has substantially limited the ability of governments to fund social protection programs and to redress imbalances in income. To eradicate this perverse outgrowth of globalization, a simple modification of the manner in which the taxable income of multinationals is calculated would allow nations injured by such practices to recover tax receipts that are legitimately due them (this would follow the method of formulary apportionment applied in treating domestic corporate taxation in the United States to prevent unfair tax competition between individual states). This means that multinationals would no longer be taxed on the basis of their declared profits in a given country (which bear no relation to the real level of sales there), but on the basis of the percentage of a corporation's actual gross sales in that country.[12] Here we have another example of a reform that is wholly feasible from the technical point of view and that could be put into effect relatively easily.

With regard to environmental protection, the most forward-looking countries are apt to be harmed by free riding on the part of neighbors and trading partners if they do not assert their authority. Nations committed to ambitious climate objectives can lessen the damage by threatening trade sanctions or instituting new tax regulations. In particular, they can refuse to sign trade agreements with countries that do not meet CO_2e emission reduction goals. The EU-Canada Comprehensive Economic and Trade Agreement (CETA), which provisionally entered into force in September 2017, does the opposite, however, by making climate protection a secondary objective by comparison with trade liberalization.

Another option is to institute a border carbon adjustment (BCA)—a levy on the carbon content of imported products—with a view to protecting domestic industry against foreign companies that are not bound by stringent targets for reducing greenhouse gas emissions. In this way an equitable relationship between domestic and foreign companies could be reestablished. A number of experts have studied the question and come to the conclusion that such a measure would not be contrary to either the letter or the spirit of international trade law, since Article 20 of the General Agreement on Tariffs and Trade (GATT), which is binding on the World Trade Organization (WTO), permits violations for the sake of protecting the environment and human life.[13]

A carbon tax of this sort has been long proposed by member countries of the European Union at summit meetings but has never won formal approval because of a lack of common political will (Germany, for example, is reluctant to annoy its trade partners outside the European Union). To circumvent this obstacle, countries that favor the measure could begin by imposing taxes on the consumption of goods having a high carbon content (cement and steel, for example), on top of existing taxes on carbon-based fuels, such as the ones discussed in Chapter 6. The fact that it could be implemented unilaterally by countries that wish to do so, and that the new levy would fall on both foreign and domestic producers, makes it a particularly attractive alternative.[14]

These examples show that states can indeed find the room for maneuver that they need in tax, social, and environmental policy, without having to hurt their international trade position (the consequences would be particularly dramatic in the case of the poorest countries). The problem lies in striking the right balance, which is to say in subordinating commercial objectives to the larger purpose of bringing about a far-reaching and durable ecological and social transition. This will require, among other things, enacting measures that prevent social and environmental standards from being lowered. Policies such as taxation of corporate profits and carbon border assessments show that countries wishing to reduce inequalities and protect the environment do not need to wait for an international consensus to be reached on these issues. They are free to act at once, and in this way create spillover effects.

In spite (or perhaps because) of their ambition, SDGs justifiably arouse a certain measure of skepticism. After all, if the promise of earlier United Nations programs had been fully realized, the world would already be a haven of peace and justice. For all their shortcomings, however, these programs can claim credit for a great deal of the progress that has been made in dealing with environmental and social problems over the past seventy years.

It is often forgotten that international policy coordination has the signal virtue of stimulating and nourishing activism at the local level. This is very clear with regard to combating biopiracy and protecting the rights of indigenous peoples—problems that were wholly neglected by the countries responsible for predation of various kinds until international conferences made it possible for local actors to make the issue a matter of domestic political debate. One thinks in particular of the Conference of the Parties (COP) to the United Nations Framework Convention on Climate Change, which meets in annual session to monitor the latest developments. The greater visibility of the climate-related activities of nongovernmental organizations, and the fact that climate change has now become a major preoccupation of world leaders, has also had a significant effect. Environmental groups are not wrong to criticize the COP for the impression its members sometimes give of being out of touch with the realities of life in much of the world's population and for the lack of effective sanctions in the event of failure to comply with agreements, but without these meetings, such groups would have no global forum for pointing out the defects of international consultation.

Coordinating these different levels of action—involving nongovernmental groups, national agencies, and international organizations—is bound to be an extremely tricky and complicated business. The policy tools available to nation-states plainly do not suffice by themselves to deal with economic and environmental inequalities, any more than the ones available to local communities do. Moreover, without action at the local level, international accords will have no force. It will therefore be necessary to harmonize initiatives at all three levels if economic and environmental inequalities are to be meaningfully addressed. Nevertheless, in spite of its limitations, its talent for delay, and its many inefficiencies, the nation-state remains the most suitable level for organizing a concerted response to the problem of distributing economic and ecological wealth. But in order to meet the dual challenge of economic inequalities and environmental crisis, a profound transformation will have to take place.

Conclusion

LET US NOW SUMMARIZE OUR FINDINGS. We started from the observation that economic inequalities are at the heart of the environmentally unsustainable predicament that poses an existential threat to the world today. It has become increasingly clear in recent decades that current levels of income and wealth inequality are neither tolerable in a democracy nor efficient from the economic point of view; that they aggravate public health risks affecting the whole of society, rich and poor alike; and that they have potentially devastating consequences for the environment.

The ominous thing is that the same trend is observed throughout the world. In most countries for which sufficiently good quality data are available, inequalities of income or inherited wealth are on the rise. And yet there is a glimmer of hope in the darkness: this increase, though it varies in extent from country to country, is essentially due to a particular set of tax, social, trade, and educational policies (or to the absence of such policies); it is therefore possible, in principle at least, to implement other policies that will reverse the trend. Contrary to what those who (consciously or unconsciously) insist on the supposedly ironclad laws of the market would have us believe, an unending escalation of social injustices is not inevitable. Inequalities are a political choice.

A detailed and coherent response to the present crisis has yet to be formulated in the United States, Europe, and the emerging countries, but already one sees the dawning of a consensus among leading figures in the social and natural sciences as well as international organizations, business, and civil society in countries throughout the world on the necessity of narrowing the new extremes of economic inequality. The development of new indicators of progress in support of this aim among the United Nations's Sustainable Development Goals is an encouraging sign, even if it is far from being sufficient.

We have also seen that if sustainable development is to be achieved we must examine another aspect of social injustice, environmental inequalities, which are intimately bound up with economic inequalities. The poor unavoidably find it harder to gain access not only to environmental resources sold through markets, such as energy and healthy foods, but also to nonmarket goods such as clean air, uncontaminated soil, and places to live that are resilient in the face of tornados, drought, and other catastrophic events. We have considered in some detail the mechanisms that create a vicious circle in which economic and environmental inequalities become mutually reinforcing. In this case the injustice is double, because the principal victims of pollution are often the ones who are least responsible for it.

Transformation on a grand scale will have to occur if present trends are to be reversed. We have seen that many policies make it possible to reduce economic disparities without increasing the pressures to which the environment is subject and the environmental inequalities that accompany them. These policies have already been put into effect in both emerging and developed countries. The transformation, if it is ever to occur, will be brought about by copying what works best in Europe, India, the United States, and elsewhere. It must be both profound and widespread. But it is within our reach.

Carrying on the transition that has now begun will require much greater efforts from all parties: researchers, who must work harder to accurately measure environmental and social inequalities with a view to understanding how they arise and why they persist; citizen associations and nongovernmental organizations, which must work harder to put the most urgent forms of injustice on the political agenda at both the national and international levels, while helping to devise solutions and put them into effect; and governments, individually and in concert, which must work harder to discover what is happening on different scales in different parts of the world, and then to act on this knowledge. Delays and setbacks will no doubt have to be overcome along the way; for just this reason, enormous quantities of ingenuity and unremitting labor will be needed if the transformation is to be fully achieved. But as I have tried to show in this short book, a way out from the vicious circle in which we are presently caught up can in fact be found. A future that will be both just and sustainable is not yet an impossibility.

NOTES

Introduction

1. The term *social-ecological state* was coined by the economist Éloi Laurent in his book *Social-écologie* (Paris: Flammarion, 2008).

1. Economic Inequality as a Component of Unsustainability

1. Thomas Piketty, *Capital in the Twenty-First Century*, trans. Arthur Goldhammer (Cambridge, MA: Belknap Press of Harvard University Press, 2014).

2. Barack Obama, "Remarks by the President on Economic Mobility," December 4, 2013, https://obamawhitehouse.archives.gov/the-press-office/2013/12/04/remarks-president-economic-mobility.

3. World Bank Group, *Poverty and Shared Prosperity 2016: Taking on Inequality* (Washington, DC: World Bank, 2016), https://elibrary.worldbank.org/doi/10.1596/978-1-4648-0958-3; Organisation for Economic Co-operation and Development, *Divided We Stand: Why Inequality Keeps Rising* (Paris: OECD, 2011); Jonathan D. Ostry, Andrew Berg, and Charalambos G. Tsangarides, "Redistribution, Inequality, and Growth," IMF Discussion Note, February 2014, https://www.imf.org/external/pubs/ft/sdn/2014/sdn1402.pdf.

4. Francis Fukuyama, *The End of History and the Last Man* (New York: Free Press, 1992).

5. David Le Blanc, "Towards Integration at Last? The Sustainable Development Goals as a Network of Targets" (working paper no. 141, UN Department of Economic and Social Affairs, April 10, 2015), https://onlinelibrary.wiley.com/doi/abs/10.1002/sd.1582.

6. Lucas Chancel, Alex Hough, and Tancrède Voituriez, "Reducing Inequalities within Countries: Assessing the Potential of the Sustainable Development Goals," *Global Policy* 9, no. 1 (2018): 5–16, https://onlinelibrary.wiley.com/toc/17585899 /2018/9/1.

7. See particularly in this connection Alain Supiot, *Grandeur et misère de l'État social* (Paris: Fayard, 2013).

8. Eric Kaufmann, "It's NOT the Economy, Stupid: Brexit as a Story of Personal Values," British Politics and Policy blog of the London School of Economics, July 7, 2016, http://eprints.lse.ac.uk/71585/.

9. Thiemo Fetzer, "Did Austerity Cause Brexit?" (CESifo Working Paper Series 7159, CESifo Group Munich, 2018); Richard Dobbs et al., "Poorer than Their Parents? A New Perspective on Income Inequality," McKinsey Global Institute Report, July 2016, https://www.mckinsey.com/featured-insights/employment-and-growth /poorer-than-their-parents-a-new-perspective-on-income-inequality.

10. See also Thomas Piketty, "Brahmin Left vs. Merchant Right: Rising Inequality and the Changing Structure of Political Conflict" (working paper 2018/7, WID. world, 2018), https://wid.world/news-article/new-paper-on-rising-inequality-and-the -changing-structure-of-political-conflict-wid-world-working-paper-2018-7/.

11. Julia Cagé, *The Price of Democracy: How Money Shapes Politics and What to Do About It,* trans. Patrick Camiller (Cambridge, MA: Harvard University Press, 2020).

12. Nolan M. McCarty, Keith T. Poole, and Howard Rosenthal, *Polarized America: The Dance of Ideology and Unequal Riches,* 2nd ed. (Cambridge, MA: MIT Press, 2016).

13. Éloi Laurent, "Inequality as Pollution, Pollution as Inequality: The Social-Ecological Nexus" (working paper, Stanford Center on Poverty and Inequality, 2013), https://inequality.stanford.edu/sites/default/files/media/_media/working_papers /laurent_inequality-pollution.pdf. See also Éloi Laurent, *Social-écologie* (Paris: Flammarion, 2011).

14. Michael Marmot and Richard G. Wilkinson, eds., *Social Determinants of Health,* 2nd ed. (Oxford: Oxford University Press, 2006).

15. Richard G. Wilkinson and Kate Pickett, *The Spirit Level: Why Equality Is Better for Everyone,* 2nd ed. (London: Penguin, 2010). See also Richard G. Wilkinson and Kate Pickett, *The Inner Level: How More Equal Societies Reduce Stress, Restore Sanity and Improve Everyone's Well-Being* (London: Penguin, 2018).

16. A visitor from Mars falls into this trap when, observing that rain falls on Earth every time umbrellas can be seen, it deduces that umbrellas are the cause of the rain. One must therefore be careful not to commit the logical fallacy *cum hoc, ergo propter hoc* (with this, therefore on account of this).

17. See, for example, Andreas Bergh, Therese Nilsson, and Daniel Waldenstrom, *Sick of Inequality? An Introduction to the Relationship between Inequality and Health* (Cheltenham, UK: Edward Elgar, 2016).

18. L. Vitetta et al., "Mind-Body Medicine: Stress and Its Impact on Overall Health and Longevity," *Annals of the New York Academy of Sciences* 1057 (December 2005): 492–505.

19. M. Kelly-Irving et al., "Childhood Adversity as a Risk for Cancer: Findings from the 1958 British Birth Cohort Study," *BMC Public Health* 13, no. 1 (2013), https://bmcpublichealth.biomedcentral.com/articles/10.1186/1471-2458-13-767.

20. Raj Chetty et al., "Where Is the Land of Opportunity? The Geography of Intergenerational Mobility in the United States" (working paper no. 19843, National Bureau of Economic Research, 2014), https://www.nber.org/papers/w19843.

21. Karla Hoff and Priyanka Pandey, "Discrimination, Social Identity, and Durable Inequalities," *American Economic Review* 96, no. 2 (2006): 206–211.

22. C. M. Steele and J. Aronson, "Stereotype Threat and the Intellectual Test Performance of African Americans," *Journal of Personality and Social Psychology* 69, no. 5 (1995): 797–811.

23. M. J. Raleigh et al., "Social and Environmental Influences on Blood Serotonin (5-HT) Concentrations in Monkeys," *Archives of General Psychiatry* 41, no. 4 (1984): 405–410.

24. James E. Zull, *The Art of Changing the Brain: Enriching Teaching by Exploring the Biology of Learning* (Sterling, VA: Stylus, 2002).

25. See, for example, Pierre Bourdieu and Jean-Claude Passeron, *Reproduction in Education, Society, and Culture,* 2nd ed., trans. Richard Nice (London: Sage, 1990).

26. S. Kuznets, "Economic Growth and Income Inequality," *American Economic Review* 45, no. 1 (1955): 1–28.

27. Piketty, *Capital in the Twenty-First Century,* 13–15, 271–274.

28. Arthur M. Okun, *Equality and Efficiency: The Big Tradeoff* (Washington, DC: Brookings Institution, 1975), 2.

29. Kaldor reasoned that, because the wealthiest save more than the poorest, the more inegalitarian a society—everything else being equal—the more it will save.

30. Nicholas Kaldor, "Capital Accumulation and Economic Growth," in *The Theory of Capital,* ed. D. C. Hague (London: Palgrave Macmillan, 1961), 177–222.

31. A. Berg et al., "Redistribution, Inequality, and Growth: New Evidence," *Journal of Economic Growth* 23, no. 3 (2018): 259.

32. Of eighteen quantitative studies using standardized data for the OECD countries over the past thirty years, half of them concluded that income inequality slowed growth, six concluded the opposite, and three reported mixed results. See

Federico Cingano, "Trends in Income Inequality and Its Impact on Economic Growth" (Social, Employment and Migration Working Papers 163, Organisation for Economic Co-operation and Development, 2014), http://www.oecd.org/els/soc/trends-in-income-inequality-and-its-impact-on-economic-growth-SEM-WP163.pdf.

33. Alain Cohn et al., "Social Comparison in the Workplace: Evidence from a Field Experiment" (discussion paper no. 5550, Institute of Labor Economics, March 2011), https://papers.ssrn.com/sol3/papers.cfm?abstract_id=1778894.

34. Emily Breza, Supreet Kaur, and Yogita Shamdasani, "The Morale Effects of Pay Inequality" (working paper no. 22491, National Bureau of Economic Research, August 2016), https://www.nber.org/papers/w22491.

35. David Card et al., "Inequality at Work: The Effect of Peer Salaries on Job Satisfaction," *American Economic Review* 102, no. 6 (2012): 2981–3003.

36. Cingano, "Trends in Income Inequality and Its Impact on Economic Growth." The implications of a study of this kind are nonetheless limited to the data it relies on. Cingano does not carefully measure income inequality at the summit of the pyramid, which is not really due to educational disadvantages.

37. Joseph E. Stiglitz, *The Price of Inequality: How Today's Divided Society Endangers Our Future* (New York: W. W. Norton, 2012).

38. Raghuram G. Rajam, *Fault Lines: How Hidden Fractures Still Threaten the World Economy,* rev. ed. (Princeton, NJ: Princeton University Press, 2011).

39. Ori Heffetz, "A Test of Conspicuous Consumption: Visibility and Income Elasticities," *Review of Economics and Statistics* 93, no. 4 (2010): 1101–1117.

40. Thorstein Veblen, *The Theory of the Leisure Class* (1899; repr., New York: Penguin, 1994).

41. Adam Smith, *The Theory of Moral Sentiments* (1759; repr., London: Penguin, 2009); Fred Hirsch, *The Social Limits to Growth,* rev. ed. (London: Routledge, 1995); Jean Baudrillard, *The Consumer Society: Myths and Structures* (1970; repr., London: Sage, 1998).

42. Samuel Bowles and Yongjin Park, "Emulation, Inequality, and Work Hours: Was Thorsten Veblen Right?," *Economic Journal* 115, no. 507 (2005): F397–F412.

43. Laurent, "Inequality as Pollution, Pollution as Inequality."

44. As a legal matter, the carbon tax was rejected by the Constitutional Council on the ground that it would create an inequality between industrial firms already bound by the European system of carbon quotas that would be subject to the tax and other firms that had been granted exemptions under the terms of the proposed legislation.

45. See, for example, Elinor Ostrom, *Governing the Commons: The Evolution of Institutions for Collective Action* (New York: Cambridge University Press, 1990).

46. In this connection see particularly Ian Gough, *Heat, Greed, and Human Need: Climate Change, Capitalism, and Sustainable Wellbeing* (Cheltenham, UK: Edward Elgar, 2017).

2. Trends and Drivers of Economic Inequality

1. Thomas Piketty, *Capital in the Twenty-First Century,* trans. Arthur Goldhammer (Cambridge, MA: Belknap Press of Harvard University Press, 2014), 16–17.

2. Thomas Blanchet, Lucas Chancel, and Amory Gethin, "How Unequal Is Europe: Evidence from Distributional National Accounts (1980–2017)" (working paper, WID.world, June 2019).

3. Anthony B. Atkinson, "On the Measurement of Inequality," *Journal of Economic Theory* 2, no. 3 (1970): 244–263.

4. The further down one goes on the social scale, the less often income is reported, and so the earnings of poorer households are liable to be underestimated as well. This source of information therefore has its own limitations. In order to have the most accurate picture possible of the overall distribution of income and wealth, tax-return data should be cross-checked against surveys wherever possible.

5. This chapter of the book is largely derived from the *World Inequality Report 2018,* which provides more details of each national inequality trajectory. See Facundo Alvaredo et al., *World Inequality Report 2018* (Cambridge, MA: Harvard University Press, 2018).

6. Karl Polyani, *The Great Transformation: The Political and Economic Origins of Our Times,* 2nd paperback ed. (Boston: Beacon Press, 2001). For a specific discussion of the US trajectory see Thomas Piketty, Emmanuel Saez, and Gabriel Zucman, "Distributional National Accounts: Methods and Estimates for the United States" (working paper no. 22945, National Bureau of Economic Research, December 2016), rev. version published in *Quarterly Journal of Economics* 133, no. 2 (2018): 553–609.

7. On the relation between capital and wealth, see Piketty, *Capital in the Twenty-First Century,* 47–49.

8. See particularly Alvaredo et al., *World Inequality Report 2018,* section 4.

9. For a detailed analysis see Piketty, *Capital in the Twenty-First Century;* Anthony B. Atkinson, *Inequality: What Can Be Done?* (Cambridge, MA: Harvard University Press, 2015); and Branko Milanović, *Global Inequality: A New Approach for the Age of Globalization* (Cambridge, MA: Belknap Press of Harvard University Press, 2016).

10. In this connection see Claudia Goldin and Lawrence F. Katz, *The Race between Technology and Education* (Cambridge, MA: Belknap Press of Harvard University Press, 2008).

11. For further discussion see Alvaredo et al., *World Inequality Report 2018*.

12. Piketty, *Capital in the Twenty-First Century*, 278–281, 314–315.

13. N. Gregory Mankiw, "Defending the One Percent," *Journal of Economic Perspectives* 26, no. 3 (2013): 21–34.

14. Alicia Ritcey, Jenn Zhao, and Anders Melin, "Snap CEO Is Crowned the King of Pay for 2017 with $505 Million," Bloomberg, May 10, 2018, https://www.bloomberg.com/graphics/2018-highest-paid-ceos/; Thomas Piketty, Emmanuel Saez, and Stephanie Stantcheva, "Optimal Taxation of Top Labor Incomes: A Tale of Three Elasticities," *American Economic Journal: Economic Policy* 6, no. 1 (2014): 230–271.

15. Paul R. Krugman, "Trade and Wages, Reconsidered," *Brookings Papers on Economic Activity* no. 1 (2008), https://www.brookings.edu/bpea-articles/trade-and-wages-reconsidered/.

16. W. F. Stolper and Paul A. Samuelson, "Protection and Real Wages," *Review of Economic Studies* 9, no. 1 (1941): 58–73.

17. Note, however, that many poor countries that reduced tariffs (such as Argentina, Chile, India, and China) saw an increase in inequality.

18. Paul R. Krugman, *Rethinking International Trade* (Cambridge, MA: MIT Press, 1994).

19. Krugman, "Trade and Wages, Reconsidered." It should be emphasized that Krugman never underestimated the effect of trade on inequality as a theoretical matter, and that, as an empirical matter, the data available in the 1990s did not point to a trade effect on inequality.

20. Thomas Philippon and Ariell Reshef, "Wages and Human Capital in the U.S. Financial Industry: 1909–2006" (working paper no. 14644, National Bureau of Economic Research, January 2009), https://www.nber.org/papers/w14644.

21. Piketty, *Capital in the Twenty-First Century*, 238–242, 350–358.

22. Julia Tanndal and Daniel Waldenström, "Does Financial Deregulation Boost Top Incomes? Evidence from the Big Bang," Centre for Economic Policy Research, February 2016, https://cepr.org/active/publications/discussion_papers/dp.php?dpno=11094.

23. Rawi Abdelal, *Capital Rules: The Construction of Global Finance* (Cambridge, MA: Harvard University Press, 2007). The term Washington Consensus refers to an ideological consensus between the governments of Ronald Reagan in the United States and Margaret Thatcher in Great Britain, at the beginning of the 1980s, subsequently transformed into a series of measures aimed at liberalizing commodity and capital markets and at reducing the role of the state in economic affairs. [On the controversy surrounding this term, see the 2004 paper by John Williamson, the English economist who coined it, "A Short History of the Washington

Consensus" (commissioned by Fundación CIDOB for "From the Washington Consensus towards a new Global Governance," Barcelona, Spain, September 24–25, 2004), https://piie.com/publications/papers/williamson0904-2.pdf.—Trans.]

24. Chancel follows Thomas Piketty in preferring the term "social state" (*l'État social*), modeled on the German *Sozialstaat,* to the Anglo-American term "welfare state" (*l'État-Providence*) on the ground that it more fully expresses the nature and scope of the various measures implemented by governments to protect and promote the well-being of their citizens; see Piketty, *Capital in the Twenty-First Century,* 477–479, 629n9.—Trans.

25. The term *predistribution* was coined by the political scientist Jacob S. Hacker in a paper titled "The Institutional Foundations of Middle-Class Democracy," *Policy Network* 6 (June 5, 2011): 33–37.

26. The attempt by the Obama administration to raise the minimum hourly wage for work performed under federal contracts was only partly successful, doing no more than restoring the wage to its 1968 level—and even then, not for all such contracts. A bill introduced by Democratic senators that would have raised the wage paid to all federal contractors from \$7.30 to \$12.00 an hour by 2020 and failed to obtain the majority of votes needed for passage. At the time of writing, the minimum wage bill to increase minimum wage to \$15 per hour, passed by House Democrats in 2019, has not been taken up by the Senate. [The Raise the Wage Act of 2019 will raise the federal minimum hourly wage to \$15.00 by 2025.—Trans.]

27. Florence Jaumotte and Carolina Osorio Buitron, "Inequality and Labor Market Institutions" (staff discussion note no. 15/14, International Monetary Fund, July 2015), https://www.imf.org/external/pubs/ft/sdn/2015/sdn1514.pdf.

28. This result was arrived at with reference to the Gini index and on the basis of survey data: "OECD Income Distribution Database (IDD): Gini, Poverty, Income, Methods and Concepts," Organisation for Economic Co-operation and Development, updated February 25, 2020, http://www.oecd.org/social/income -distribution-database.htm.

29. Isabelle Joumard, Mauro Pisu, and Debbie Bloch, "Tackling Income Inequality: The Role of Taxes and Transfers," *OECD Journal: Economic Studies* (2012): 1–34.

30. Organisation for Economic Co-operation and Development, "Focus on Top Incomes and Taxation in OECD Countries: Was the Crisis a Game Changer?," May 2014, http://www.oecd.org/social/OECD2014-FocusOnTopIncomes.pdf.

31. Fabien Dell, Thomas Piketty, and Emmanuel Saez, "Income and Wealth Concentration in Switzerland over the 20th Century" (discussion paper no. 5090,

Centre for Economic Policy Research, May 2005), https://cepr.org/active/publications/discussion_papers/dp.php?dpno=5090.

32. Piketty, Saez, and Stantcheva, "Optimal Taxation of Top Labor Incomes."

33. Organisation for Economic Co-operation and Development, "Focus on Top Incomes and Taxation in OECD Countries."

34. Quoted in "In Class Warfare, Guess Which Class Is Winning," *New York Times*, November 26, 2006.

35. Martin Gilens and Benjamin I. Page, "Testing Theories of American Politics: Elites, Interest Groups, and Average Citizens," *Perspectives on Politics* 12, no. 3 (2014): 564–581.

36. Emmanuel Saez and Gabriel Zucman, *The Triumph of Injustice* (New York: Norton, 2019).

37. Lucas Chancel and Thomas Spencer, "Greasing the Wheel: Oil's Role in the Global Crisis," Vox: Centre for Economic Policy Research Policy Portal, May 16, 2012, https://voxeu.org/article/greasing-wheel-oil-s-role-global-crisis.

38. Robert K. Kaufmann et al., "Do Household Energy Expenditures Affect Mortgage Delinquency Rates?," *Energy Economics* 22, no. 2 (2011): 188–194.

39. See particularly Milanović, *Global Inequality.*

40. Mariana Mazzucato, *The Entrepreneurial State: Debunking Public vs. Private Sector Myths,* rev. ed. (New York: Public Affairs, 2015).

41. Facundo Alvaredo et al., "The Elephant Curve of Global Inequality and Growth," *American Economic Association Papers and Proceedings* 108 (2018): 103–108.

3. Unequal Access to Environmental Resources

1. See for instance N. Stern, *The Economics of Climate Change: The Stern Review* (Cambridge: Cambridge University Press, 2007), https://doi.org/10.1017/CBO9780511817434.

2. Éloi Laurent, "Issues in Environmental Justice within the European Union," *Ecological Economics* 70, no. 11 (2011): 1846–1853.

3. Christine Liddell and Chris Morris, "Fuel Poverty and Human Health: A Review of Recent Evidence," *Energy Policy* 38, no. 6 (2010): 2987–2997.

4. Robert K. Kaufmann et al., "Do Household Energy Expenditures Affect Mortgage Delinquency Rates?," *Energy Economics* 22, no. 2 (2011): 188–194.

5. This, of course, is an average figure; a hunter-gatherer who spent most of the day outdoors needed to consume a larger number of calories than a sedentary person today.

6. In this example, all the energy consumed by slaves is attributed to their master—a not unreasonable assumption since in many cases they were worked to death. I shall not enter here into a discussion of the degree of servitude or coercion under which the builders of the pyramids labored. Authorities agree that while slavery did not exist in Egypt before the Ptolemaic period, there were several forms of servitude, including corvée (an obligation imposed on everyone in the case of large public works projects, notably irrigation and royal monuments) and forced labor (for ordinary convicts). Otherwise I assume that an ass consumed 10 kWh per day and that no other source of energy was exploited. This is no doubt an oversimplification, but it nonetheless supplies us with a reasonable order of magnitude for purposes of comparison.

7. See the rigorous reconstruction by Glen P. Peters and Edgar G. Hertwich, "CO_2 Embodied in International Trade with Implications for Global Climate Policy," *Environmental Science and Technology* 42, no. 5 (2008): 1401–1407.

8. Prabodh Pourouchottamin et al., "New Representations of Energy Consumption," *Cahiers du Club d'Ingénerie Prospective Énergie et Environment* 22 (October 2013), https://www.researchgate.net/publication/326476019_New_representations_of _energy_consumptionCLIP_Les_cahiers_du_Club_d%27Ingenierie_Prospective _Energie_et_Environnement_number_22_October_2013.

9. Jihoon Minh and Narasimha D. Rao, "Estimating Uncertainty in Household Energy Footprints: The Cases of Brazil and India," *Journal of Industrial Ecology* 22, no. 6 (2017): 1307–1317.

10. World Health Organization, "Water Sanitation Hygiene: What Is the Minimum Quantity of Water Needed?" (2013), https://www.who.int/water_sanitation _health/emergencies/qa/emergencies_qa5/en/.

11. A. Y. Hoekstra and A. K. Chapagain, "Water Footprints of Nations: Water Use by People as a Function of Their Consumption Pattern," *Water Resources Management* 21, no. 1 (2007): 35–48.

12. In India and China, where a great majority of the population lives in areas regularly subject to water shortages, one of the factors aggravating the situation is the reduction in the size of mountain glaciers, which, under the effect of climate change, creates shortages in the valleys below. This phenomenon, observed not only in the Himalayas but also in the Andes, will become still more pronounced in the years to come.

13. Kate Bayliss and Rehema Tukai, "Services and Supply Chains: The Role of the Domestic Private Sector in Water Service Delivery in Tanzania" (United Nations Development Program publication, October 2011), http://www.undp.org

/content/dam/undp/library/Poverty%20Reduction/Inclusive%20development
/Tanzania-Water.pdf.

14. Institut national de la santé et de la recherche médical, *Inégalités sociales de santé en lien avec l'alimentation et l'activité physique* (Paris: Les éditions Inserm, 2014). While the prevalence of obesity among children has recently leveled out—something that is usually reported as good news—stabilization has occurred because of a widening of income gaps: the children of the richest are less and less overweight, the children of the poorest more and more overweight.

15. Karl Polanyi, *The Great Transformation: The Political and Economic Origins of Our Times*, 2nd paperback ed. (Boston: Beacon Press, 2001), 36–41.

16. Karl Marx, "Debates on the Law on Thefts of Wood," *Rheinische Zeitung* (October–November 1842), reprinted in Karl Marx and Friedrich Engels, *Collected Works*, 50 vols. (New York: International Publishers, 1975–2004), 1:224–263.

17. Juan Martínez Alier, *The Environmentalism of the Poor: A Study of Ecological Conflicts and Valuation* (Northampton, MA: Edward Elgar, 2002).

4. Unequal Exposure to Environmental Risks

1. Stéphane Hallegatte et al., *Shock Waves: Managing the Impacts of Climate Change on Poverty* (Washington, DC: World Bank Group, 2016).

2. Michael Marmot and Richard G. Wilkinson, eds., *Social Determinants of Health,* 2nd ed. (Oxford: Oxford University Press, 2006).

3. Stephen M. Rappaport and Martyn T. Smith, "Environment and Disease Risks," *Science* 330, no. 6003 (2010): 460–461.

4. For an early official report see "Siting of Hazardous Waste Landfills and Their Correlation with Racial and Economic Status of Surrounding Communities," US Government Accounting Office, June 1983, https://www.gao.gov/products /RCED-83-168. See also Seema Arora and Timothy N. Cason, "Do Community Characteristics Determine Environmental Outcomes? Evidence from the Toxic Release Inventory," *Southern Economic Journal* 65, no. 4 (1999): 691–716.

5. Anna Aizer et al., "Lead Exposure and Racial Disparities in Test Scores" (working paper, Brown University, February 2015), https://economics.yale.edu /sites/default/files/aizer_feb_12_2015.pdf.

6. Saturnism affects fewer than 0.1 percent of children in France today, a rate twenty times lower than in the 1990s.

7. Heather M. Stapleton et al., "Serum PBDEs in a North Carolina Toddler Cohort: Associations with Handwipes, House Dust, and Socioeconomic Variables," *Environmental Health Perspectives* 120, no. 7 (2012): 1049–1054.

8. See the WHO update on ambient air pollution: "Mortality and Burden of Disease from Ambient Air Pollution," World Health Organization, https://www .who.int/gho/phe/outdoor_air_pollution/burden/en/, accessed April 2020.

9. The hair in question is assumed to have a thickness of one hundred microns, a little thicker than the human average of about seventy microns.

10. To arrive at these figures, researchers at the national public health agency used a well-established causal relationship between fine-particle pollution and mortality in rich countries: when $PM_{2.5}$ levels increase by ten micrograms per cubic meter of air, the risk of death is 7 percent higher, other things being equal. See M. Pascal et al., "Impacts de l'exposition chronique aux particules fines sur la mortalité en France continentale et analyse des gains en santé de plusieurs scénarios de réduction de la pollution atmosphérique," *Santé publique France* (June 2016), http://invs .santepubliquefrance.fr/Publications-et-outils/Portail-documentaire.

11. Adrian Wilson et al., "Coal Blooded: Putting Profits before People," Indigenous Environmental Network, Little Village Environmental Justice Organization, National Association for the Advancement of Colored People, 2012, https://www .naacp.org/wp-content/uploads/2016/04/Coal_Blooded_Executive_Summary _Update.pdf. See also C. G. Schneider and M. Padian, "Dirty Air, Dirty Power: Mortality and Health Damage due to Air Pollution from Power Plants," Clean Air Task Force, 2004, https://www.catf.us/resources/publications/view/24.

12. Séverine Deguen et al., "Neighbourhood Characteristics and Long-Term Air Pollution Levels Modify the Association between the Short-Term Nitrogen Dioxide Concentrations and All-Cause Mortality in Paris," *PLOS One* 10, no. 7 (2015), https://journals.plos.org/plosone/article?id=10.1371/journal.pone .0131463.

13. "Burden of Disease from Household Air Pollution for 2012: Summary of Results," World Health Organization, 2014, https://www.who.int/phe/health_topics /outdoorair/databases/FINAL_HAP_AAP_BoD_24March2014.pdf.

14. The increase in the risk of contracting these diseases ranges from 12 to 28 percent, depending on the agricultural population considered; see the report issued by the Institut national de la santé et de la recherche médicale, *Pesticides: Effets sur la santé* (Paris: INSERM, 2013).

15. This is particularly the case in France, as well as other countries in Europe and North America; it is probably also the case in the rural areas of many emerging countries where health information and access to medical care are more difficult to obtain than in urban areas.

16. Juan Martínez Alier, *The Environmentalism of the Poor: A Study of Ecological Conflicts and Valuation* (Northampton, MA: Edward Elgar, 2002).

17. E. M. Fischer and R. Knutti, "Anthropogenic Contribution to Global Occurrence of Heavy-Precipitation and High-Temperature Extremes," *Nature Climate Change* 5, no. 6 (2015): 560–564.

18. David Simon and Eric Overmyer, creators, *Treme,* aired 2010–2013, on HBO.

19. François Gemenne, "What's in a Name: Social Vulnerabilities and the Refugee Controversy in the Wake of Hurricane Katrina," in *Environment, Forced Migration, and Social Vulnerability,* ed. Tamer Afifi and Jill Jäger (New York: Springer, 2010), 29–40.

20. Gordon Walker and Kate Burningham, "Flood Risk, Vulnerability and Environmental Justice: Evidence and Evaluation of Inequality in a UK Context," *Critical Social Policy* 31, no. 2 (2011): 216–240.

21. Hallegatte et al., *Shock Waves.*

5. Unequal Responsibility for Pollution

1. Simon L. Lewis and Mark A. Maslin, "Defining the Anthropocene," *Nature* 519 (2015): 171–180.

2. Nicholas Stern, *The Economics of Climate Change: The Stern Review* (Cambridge: Cambridge University Press, 2007).

3. Lucas Chancel and Thomas Piketty, "Carbon and Inequality: From Kyoto to Paris; Trends in the Global Inequality of Carbon Emissions (1998–2013) and Prospects for an Equitable Adaptation Fund," Paris School of Economics, November 3, 2015, http://piketty.pse.ens.fr/files/ChancelPiketty2015.pdf.

4. See Gene M. Grossman and Alan B. Krueger, "Economic Growth and the Environment," *Quarterly Journal of Economics* 110, no. 2 (1995): 353–377.

5. David I. Stern, Michael S. Common, and Edward B. Barbier, "Economic Growth and Environmental Degradation: The Environmental Kuznets Curve and Sustainable Development," *World Development* 24, no. 7 (1996): 1151–1160. See also Diana Ivanova et al., "Environmental Impact Assessment of Household Consumption," *Journal of Industrial Ecology* 20, no. 3 (2016): 526–536.

6. See for example Manfred Lenzen et al., "A Comparative Multivariate Analysis of Household Energy Requirements in Australia, Brazil, Denmark, India, and Japan," *Energy* 31, no. 2 (2006): 181–207.

7. Fabrice Lenglart, Christophe Lesieur, and Jean-Louis Pasquier, "Les émissions de CO_2 du circuit économique en France," in *L'Économie française: Comptes et dossiers* (Paris: INSEE, 2010), 101–125; Jane Golley and Xin Meng, "Income Inequality and Carbon Dioxide Emissions: The Case of Chinese Urban Households," *Energy Economics* 34, no. 6 (2012): 1864–1872.

8. Chancel and Piketty, "Carbon and Inequality." The median-income CO_2e elasticity value we use for the United States, 0.9 percent, is close to the result of 0.6 percent obtained by Kevin Ummel, "Who Pollutes? A Household-Level Database of America's Greenhouse Gas Footprint" (working paper no. 381, Center for Global Development, October 2014), https://www.cgdev.org/publication/who -pollutes-household-level-database-americas-greenhouse-gas-footprint -working-paper.

9. Prabodh Pourouchottamin et al., "New Representations of Energy Consumption," *Cahiers du Club d'Ingénerie Prospective Énergie et Environnement* 22 (October 2013), https://www.researchgate.net/publication/326476019_New_representations_of _energy_consumptionCLIP_Les_cahiers_du_Club_d%27Ingenierie_Prospective _Energie_et_Environnement_number_22_October_2013.

10. Lucas Chancel, "Are Younger Generations Higher Carbon Emitters than Their Elders? Inequalities, Generations, and CO_2 Emissions in France and in the USA," *Ecological Economics* 100 (April 2014): 195–207.

11. Jean-Pierre Nicolas and Damien Verry, "A Socioeconomic and Spatial Analysis to Explain Greenhouse Gas Emissions due to Individual Travels" (presented paper, RGS-IBG Annual International Conference 2015, University of Exeter).

12. My 2014 paper (see note 10 above) deals with direct emissions, but it is very probable that its conclusions would have been strengthened if indirect emissions had been analyzed as well. Unfortunately, owing to a lack of data, this was not possible. Although I measure the generational effect using temporal trend analysis, this does not skew the results because per capita direct emissions began to fall in the late 1970s.

13. It is worth pointing out here that low-cost flights did not exist in the 1970s and that young people today travel by airplane more often than their parents did at the same age. Nevertheless, considering direct emissions as a whole (air travel included), this effect seems not to be decisive—at least not up until 2005, the last date for which I measured emissions. Recall too that, per kilometer and per passenger, an old car with two passengers consumes only a little less energy than a medium-range airplane (about 80–100g CO_2e / km-passenger as opposed to 100–120g CO_2e / km-passenger).

14. The report that launched the debate, *Hiding behind the Poor,* was published in October 2007 by the Indian branch of Greenpeace. For a summary see Shoibal Chakravarty and M. V. Ramana, "The Hiding behind the Poor Debate: A Synthetic Overview," in *Handbook of Climate Change and India: Development, Politics, and Governance,* ed. Navroz K. Dubash (New Delhi: Oxford University Press, 2012), 218–229.

15. Shoibal Chakravarty et al., "Sharing Global CO$_2$ Emission Reductions among One Billion High Emitters," *Proceedings of the National Academy of Sciences* 106, no. 29 (2009): 11884–11888.

6. Reducing Inequalities in a Finite World

1. Interview with Homi Kharas, "Émergence d'une classe moyenne mondiale et d'une économie à faible émission de carbon," Regards sur la terre, October 21, 2016, http://regardssurlaterre.com/emergence-dune-classe-moyenne-mondiale-et -dune-economie-faible-emission-de-carbone.

2. Éloi Laurent, "Inequality as Pollution, Pollution as Inequality: The Social-Ecological Nexus" (working paper, Stanford Center on Poverty and Inequality, 2013).

3. My analysis is available via www.lucaschancel.info/hup.

4. N. Poize and A. Rüdinger, "Projets citoyens pour la production d'énergie renouvelable: Une comparaison France-Allemagne" (working paper, Institut du développement durable et des relations internationales [IDDRI] January 2014), http://www.iddri.org/Publications/Projets-citoyens-pour-la-production-d -energie-renouvelable-unecomparaison-France-Allemagne.

5. Mildred E. Warner, "Privatization Does Not Yield Cost Savings," in *Reclaiming Public Water: Achievements, Struggles, and Visions from around the World*, ed. Brid Brennan et al., 2nd ed. (Amsterdam: Transnational Institute / Brussels: Corporate Europe Observatory, 2005), http://www.tni.org/tnibook/reclaimingpublicwater2.

6. Brid Brennan et al., "Empowering Public Water: Ways Forward," concluding essay in *Reclaiming Public Water*.

7. Robin Carruthers, Malise Dick, and Anuja Saurkar, "Affordability of Public Transport in Developing Countries" (transport paper TP-3, World Bank, Washington, DC, 2005), https://openknowledge.worldbank.org/handle/10986/17408.

8. Uri Dadush and Shimelse Ali, "In Search of the Global Middle Class: A New Index," Carnegie Endowment for International Peace, July 23, 2012, https:// carnegieendowment.org/2012/07/23/in-search-of-global-middle-class-new-index -pub-48908.

9. Blandine Barreau and Anne Dujin, "Comment limiter l'effet rebond des politiques d'efficacité énergétique dans le logement?: L'importance des incitations comportementales" (Note d'analyse 320, France Stratégie, 2013), http://archives .strategie.gouv.fr/cas/en/system/files/2013-02-05-incitationcomportementalesec onomieenergie-na320.html.

10. Timothée Erard, Lucas Chancel, and Mathieu Saujot, "La précarité énergétique face au défi des données" (working paper, IDDRI, April 2013), https://www

.iddri.org/fr/publications-et-evenements/etude/la-precarite-energetique-face-au
-defi-des-donnees.

11. The term *social-ecological state* is due to Éloi Laurent, who introduced it in
Social-écologie (Paris: Flammarion, 2008).

12. Lucas Chancel, "Quel bouclier social-énergétique?" (working paper, IDDRI,
July 2013), https://www.iddri.org/fr/publications-et-evenements/document-de
-travail/quel-bouclier-social-energetique.

13. See, for example, Robert Pollin, James Heintz, and Heidi Garrett-Peltier,
"The Economic Benefits of Investing in Clean Energy: How the Economic Stim-
ulus Program and New Legislation Can Boost U.S. Economic Growth and Employment," Center for American Progress / PERI, June 2009, https://www.peri
.umass.edu/fileadmin/pdf/other_publication_types/green_economics/economic
_benefits/economic_benefits.PDF.

14. A. C. Pigou, *The Economics of Welfare* (London: Macmillan, 1920).

15. If indirect health costs are taken into account, fossil fuel subsidies cost
governments fifteen times more, roughly $5 trillion per year, according to the
International Monetary Fund. See "Counting the Cost of Energy Subsidies," International Monetary Fund Survey, July 17, 2015, https://www.imf.org/en/News
/Articles/2015/09/28/04/53/sonew070215a.

16. Thomas Sterner, ed., *Fuel Taxes and the Poor: The Distributional Effects of Gasoline Taxation and Their Implications for Climate Policy* (London: Routledge,
2012).

17. "Fossil Fuel Subsidies in Indonesia: Trends, Impacts, and Reforms," Asian
Development Bank, 2015, https://www.adb.org/sites/default/files/publication
/175444/fossil-fuel-subsidies-indonesia.pdf.

18. See, for example, Jean-Charles Hourcade and Emmanuel Combet, *Fis-
calité carbone et finance climat: Un contrat social pour notre temps* (Paris: Les
Petits Matins, 2017).

19. In the original French edition of this book, written before the rise of the
yellow vests movement, I noted that while the issue of equity had not yet surfaced
in the debate over a carbon tax in France, it would eventually if policymakers did
not design ambitious programs to assist low-income households; see *Insoutenables
inégalités: Pour une justice sociale et environnementale* (Paris: Les petits matins,
2017), 150–152.

20. "Evaluation du budget 2019," Institut des Politiques Publiques, October 11,
2018, https://www.ipp.eu/en/news/11-oct-evaluating-the-2019-budget/.

21. Lucas Chancel, Damien Demailly, and Felix Sieker, "Inequalities and the
Environment: A Review of Applied Policy Research," *IDDRI Study* 6 (October 2015),

https://www.iddri.org/sites/default/files/PDF/Publications/Catalogue%20Iddri/Etude/201510-ST0615-inegalites%20think%20tanks.pdf.

22. Lucas Chancel and Thomas Piketty, "Carbon and Inequality: From Kyoto to Paris; Trends in the Global Inequality of Carbon Emissions (1998–2013) and Prospects for an Equitable Adaptation Fund," Paris School of Economics, November 3, 2015, http://piketty.pse.ens.fr/files/ChancelPiketty2015.pdf.

23. Julien Caudeville, Nathalie Velly, and Martin Ramel, "Retour d'expérience des travaux de caractérisation des inégalités environnementales en région," Rapport d'étude pour le Ministère de l'Environnement, de l'Énergie et de la Mer, INERIS, February 2016, https://www.ineris.fr/sites/ineris.fr/files/contribution/Documents/drc-15-152407-12400a-rex-vf2-1465459131.pdf.

24. It will be recalled that French law was reformed after the Second World War in reaction against the use of personal files by the Vichy regime under Nazi occupation. A certain resistance to change with regard to the collection and use of private information is therefore perfectly understandable.

25. Leonardo Trasande, Patrick Malecha, and Teresa Attina, "Particulate Matter Exposure and Preterm Birth: Estimates of U.S. Attributable Burden and Economic Costs," *Environmental Health Prospect* 124, no. 12 (2016): 1913–1918.

26. A 2015 French Senate report estimated total costs to be as much as three times higher; see "Air Pollution Costs France 100 Billion Euros per Year," Phys.org, July 15, 2015, https://phys.org/news/2015-07-air-pollution-france-billion-euros.html.

27. See Chancel and Piketty, "Carbon and Inequality."

7. Local Organization vs. International Coordination

1. Rob Hopkins, *The Transition Handbook: From Oil Dependency to Local Resilience* (White River Junction, VT: Chelsea Green, 2008).

2. Luc Semal, "Le militantisme écologiste face à l'imaginaire collectif: Le cas des villes en transition," in *Pour une socio-anthropologie de l'environnement,* ed. Sophie Poirot-Delpech and Laurence Raineau, 2 vols. (Paris: L'Harmattan, 2012), 2:199–210.

3. Paul Ricoeur, *The Course of Recognition,* trans. David Pellauer (Cambridge, MA: Harvard University Press, 2005).

4. Edward B. Barbier, "Hurricane Katrina's Lessons for the World," *Nature* 524, no. 7565 (2015): 285–287.

5. Alain Supiot, *Grandeur et misère de l'État social* (Paris: Fayard, 2013).

6. It should be emphasized that in this case the sums reassigned correspond to the share of the tax on gross income that the state would have collected from the

donor had the donation not been made. One can easily imagine a system in which the state's contribution exceeds 25 percent.

7. According to a June 2018 Climate Action Network Europe report, no European country has met the goals agreed to in Paris: "Off Target: Ranking of EU Countries' Ambition and Progress in Fighting Climate Change," http://www.caneurope .org/docman/climate-energy-targets/3357-off-target-ranking-of-eu-countries -ambition-and-progress-in-fighting-climate-change/file.

8. Joseph E. Stiglitz, Amartya Sen, and Jean-Paul Fitoussi, "Rapport de la Commission sur la mesure des performances économiques et du progrès social," Ministère de l'Économie, de l'Industrie et de l'Emploi, Paris, September 2009, https://www.ladocumentationfrancaise.fr/rapports-publics/094000427/index .shtml. An English version of the report, commissioned by the French government under Nicolas Sarkozy, is available via https://ec.europa.eu/eurostat/documents /118025/118123/Fitoussi+Commission+report.

9. The United Kingdom, a pioneer in this field, is nonetheless an exception: its set of more than thirty "well-being" indicators includes no explicit measure of inequalities of income or inherited wealth.

10. "Inequality in Asia and the Pacific in the Era of the 2030 Agenda for Sustainable Development," Economic and Social Commission for Asia and the Pacific, May 7, 2018, https://www.unescap.org/publications/inequality-asia-and-pacific-era -2030-agenda-sustainable-development.

11. Gabriel Zucman, *The Hidden Wealth of Nations: The Scourge of Tax Havens,* trans. Teresa Lavender Fagan (Chicago: University of Chicago Press, 2015).

12. Ibid.

13. See, for example, Jennifer Hillman, "Changing Climate for Carbon Taxes: Who's Afraid of the WTO?" (Climate and Energy Paper Series 2013, German Marshall Fund of the United States), https://www.scribd.com/document/155956625 /Changing-Climate-for-Carbon-Taxes-Who-s-Afraid-of-the-WTO.

14. Karsten Neuhoff et al., "Inclusion of Consumption of Carbon Intensive Materials in Emissions Trading: An Option for Carbon Trading Post-2020," Climate Strategies Report, May 2016, http://www.lse.ac.uk/GranthamInstitute/wp -content/uploads/2016/06/CS-Report.pdf. The quota system presently in force in Europe applies to the level of production, and then only to producers based within the European Union. A tax on consumption has the advantage of applying to all producers, even those abroad.

ACKNOWLEDGMENTS

I owe special thanks to Tancrède Voituriez and Thomas Piketty, whose teaching and research (including a number of projects on which we worked together) inspired me to write this book. I would also like to thank my colleagues at IDDRI with whom I have collaborated on other projects cited in this work, particularly Michel Colombier, Claude Henry, Teresa Ribera, Mathieu Saujot, and Laurence Tubiana, as well as my colleagues at the World Inequality Lab. Thanks, too, to Louis Chauvel, Prabodh Pourrouchottamin, Narasimha Rao, and Julia Steinberger for their comments. I am grateful to Marie-Edith Alouf, Dominique Chancel, and Aurore Lalucq for their careful proof-reading. My thanks, finally, to my family and friends, to Alexandra for her endless patience, and to Kevin Jamey and Simon Ilse for their inexhaustible energy.

INDEX